extreme spiritual
makeover

reflecting the heart of Christ
in my priorities

By Kris Goertzen

extreme spiritual makeover

reflecting the heart of Christ
in my priorities

By Kris Goertzen

For more information about Kris Goertzen Ministries, please visit her at:

www.krisgoertzen.com

Thank you, Mom

not only for being the first one to introduce me to the heart of God,
but for promising me that life near Christ would have
boundless adventure and joy.
You were so right!

Thank you, Dad

for leaving me with your striking example of integrity.
I still hear your voice instructing me in it everyday.
I hope I'm still making you proud.

Thank you, Elizabeth George, for helping me see my life through a
Biblical grid of goals and priorities.

Thank you, Brenda Smart , for doing all the work so I could first teach this to
our dear ladies at Grace Bible Church in Hutchinson, KS.

But mostly, thank you, Rick, Bethany, Sarah, and Joshua, for your steadfast love
and patience at my feeble attempts to reflect the heart of Christ in our home.

Table of Contents

Introduction

I'm thrilled you're joining me for your very own Extreme Spiritual Makeover!

It's **Extreme** because that's what God deserves from each of us. Extreme effort, extreme obedience, extreme love!

It's **Spiritual** because the only life worth living flows from the Holy Spirit's supernatural power working in our hearts to reflect the beauty of Christ!

It's a **Makeover** because we need a total transformation that begins in our heart, not a slight alteration, but a *complete change* from the inside out!

As a brand new believer, I'll never forget the intense thirst I had to live my new life in Christ to the fullest. More than my next breath, I wanted my life to count for Christ...but I didn't know how! I was certain that God deserved more from my life than a warm pew on Sunday mornings. I desperately prayed that God would give me someone to show me how to make my life count for Him. I didn't want to flounder though my Christian life and I didn't want ordinary. Before I even knew the words; "mentor" or "discipler" I was begging God to send me such a woman who would teach me how to live entirely for Him.

To my great delight, God answered the cry of my heart! It took 5 long years of waiting, but He finally gave me an incredible spiritual friend to show me how to live God's priorities for my life. I'm a completely different woman because Elizabeth George took me in. She spilled wisdom from her walk with God on me, the life-giving water of the Word to my parched heart. And now many years later, I get to pass on these tremendous truths that have been transforming my life to women like you who also want to live near the heart of Christ. That make you a ministry dream come true!

My desire is to give women like you and I, practical ideas to help us take God's Word from the *knowing* of truth to *living* it every moment of every day! And as we do, may we bring God all the glory He deserves!

Warning!

Before we go any further I need to warn you that there's tremendous power in this study! It's the power to change! So many of my girlfriends have been *radically* changed by this study, not from my words, (don't be silly!) but from God's. If you do this study properly, if you dig into God's Word and ask Him for courage to honestly look into your own heart, you, my friend, are going to change! But, don't be afraid! Don't let Satan rob you of your hope for a better, more godly life. We're going to need every ounce of God's power if we're going to get ourselves out of the ruts we're in and become the women God dreams us to be. We'll be women driven by His priorities.

If you're like me, you *know* you should work on some things, but you're a bit comfy in the rut you've been in and don't really want to do the work it's going to take. Part of you wants to live with a single-minded passion for Christ, while the other part is content right where you are. Like, I half want to be thin and half want to eat an entire chocolate truffle cheesecake!

We both better stop right now and ask God to ignite a passion for Him that completely overwhelms any other desire in our hearts! Let's ask Him to use this Extreme Spiritual Makeover to change us forever!

Take a moment to write out a prayer of commitment that gives the Holy Spirit your consent for open heart surgery, to do whatever it takes to reflect the beauty of Christ to a dark and dying world.

> *"Search me, O God, and know my heart;*
> *Try me and know my anxious thoughts;*
> *And see if there be any hurtful way in me,*
> *And lead me in the everlasting way."*
> *Psalm 139:23, 24*

Lord, I invite you to work in my heart. Open my eyes to see your glorious truth.

Now, my friend, you're ready for your very own Extreme Spiritual Makeover! I predict that you'll be so radically transformed by faithfully applying the scriptures and principles found inside this book that others may not even recognize you!

We're going to lay the details of your life beside God's Word and see the wonderful things He has waiting for you! We're going to evaluate, dream and plan together. We're going to discover God's goals and priorities for your life, then plan steps together to reach them!

And because I care *deeply* about your spiritual journey, I have such a special gift for you! I've made 6 videos to go along with this study as my *free gift* to you! I made you one introduction video that'll bring you into my personal story, and 5 more videos to watch before you begin each new section. Each video is designed to take you on a deeper dive into each priority and give you oodles of giggles and encouragement along the way! By the time I tell you all my stories and give you Biblical context for each priority, they're each about 45 minutes. Email me at info@krisgoertzen.com and I'll send you a link right away!

There's so much ahead of us, let's get started on a fresh, life-long journey of reflecting the heart of Christ in our priorities! I'm cheering you on...

with all my heart,

Heavenly Father,
This dear woman longs to reflect You in every part of her life. That desire surely delights
Your heart. Please pour out Your Holy Spirit on her as she daily opens Your Word. Shout
Your love and Your instruction to her. Give her a glimpse of Your dear Son that will
compel her to live for Him as she's never lived before! Burn away every sin that mars
her reflection of Christ. Your Word tells us that You are a God of fresh starts and second
chances. Use this study to dramatically bless her and all those within her reach,
for Your honor and Your glory.
Rule and reign fully in her heart,
for Jesus sake, Amen.

Chapter One

Priority Number One
A Heart Consumed with God

Heart-Verse

*"Thus says the LORD, Heaven is My throne and the earth is My footstool.
Where then is a house you could build for Me?
And where is a place that I may rest? For My hand made all these things,
Thus all these things came into being, declares the LORD.
But to this one will I look,
To him who is humble and contrite of spirit,
and who trembles at My Word."*

Isaiah 66:1, 2

Priority Number One
A Heart Consumed With God

It's fascinating how I complicate my Christian life! I have immense lists of expectations for myself. I have weighty lists of do's and don'ts, shoulds and shouldn'ts, secretly hoping they'll impress my Heavenly Father. I guess that's why our Heart-Verse is so precious to me. Let's take it apart line by line.

"Heaven is My throne and the earth is My footstool."

What an incredible picture! As if the great God of Heaven, the Sovereign of the universe who dwells in unapproachable light has leaned back in satisfaction and crossed His ankles to rest His feet on planet earth. The point seems inescapable! He is so great. We are so small.

This is the picture I need to carry with me when I begin to get too big for my britches and when I want the world to revolve around me. It's good for me to be reminded that I'm not God. It's embarrassing to admit, but sometimes I act like I am.

"Where then is a house you could build for Me?
And where is a place that I may rest? For My hand made all these things,
Thus all these things came into being, declares the LORD."

I remember how fun it was to make my daddy proud. I would sit quietly in church, show respect to others, do well in school, all to hear that he was proud of me. I loved him dearly and there was nothing I wanted more in the world!

All that transferred over to my Heavenly Father when I began to follow Christ. I worked feverishly to make Him proud. Even in my first prayer as a believer I vowed to not be one of those people who just warms a pew on Sunday morning. I wanted to be busy in Kingdom work and bring Him lots of glory.

And then one day a quote by John Piper hit me square between the eyes. It goes like this…

"God is most glorified in you, when you are most satisfied in Him."

I was stunned.

I'd been doing all manner of busy work for the Lord with all the perfection I could muster. And that was the problem. I was doing, not being. I was working not enjoying. Like feverishly running around organizing closets, doing laundry, and mopping floors while my precious babies just wanted to sit next to me and cuddle. Like Mary and Martha. I was giving my best energy to the wrong things.

He wants me to realize that I can't build anything to impress the Creator God. He doesn't need me to frantically build Him a Pinterest perfect family, or a large impressive ministry. He's very clear that He'll take care of those things.

Now, my dear friend, let's take a look at what He does want!

"But to this one will I look,
To him who is humble and contrite of spirit, and who trembles at My Word."

It brings me to tears every time. He wants me. He wants you!

He's looking for someone who will just stop all the frenetic activity and all the long to-do lists. He's longing for women who will linger long with Him, who will offer up their hearts to Him and love Him enough to listen intently and joyfully carry out His wishes without all the distractions of our own.

Without a doubt our Extreme Spiritual Makeover begins with loving God for who He is and what He's done! My dream is that we'll linger with Him and be enamored by His boundless love for us. I'm convinced we cannot love a God we do not know. So let's put all the distractions down and be in awe of His Word.

A.W. Tozer has said, *"Without doubt, the mightiest thought the mind can entertain is the thought of God."*

I wonder if we assume too easily that we know God or love Him. Those words can come rolling off our tongues without the slightest awe or reverence. The most strenuous effort of our lives must be to know God. This goal, this lifelong passion must become increasingly more evident in our lives. Knowing and loving God is our highest endeavor. Without this kind of love for Him, our lives will fester with sin, and that sin will permeate us.

Our goal can be the same as Oswald Chambers, *"My goal is God Himself, not joy, nor peace, nor even blessing, but Himself, my God."*

When was the last time you *really* paused to consider God's love for *you*? Let's take a deep, cleansing breath and spend some time talking about that!

Do you know He sees you as irresistibly beautiful? Before Christ you were naked, marred, and filthy. When you cried out for Christ's forgiveness, God came to you and clothed you with Christ's beautiful righteousness. In His sight you're a most beautiful treasure. Take moment and savor that!

Before time began He made provision for you to become His. God set *you* in His eternal mind and heart and decided that He would buy you out of slavery to sin at a sacrifice so great and costly, therefore, we must conclude that you are incomparably precious to Him.

Now that you're His precious, adopted child, think of all He's provided for you! All the grace and blessing you'll *ever* need. Do you realize angels aren't so precious to God as you? Your love for Him is sweeter, your obedience and sacrifice more fragrant, your voice more melodious than all the angels of heaven!

At the moment you saw that glimpse of His beauty and worth, when you exchanged all that you were for all that He is, He sealed His love for you by filling you with Himself! His Spirit resides in you and continues to draw you where He wants you which is closer and closer to Him. Now, you're never, even for a moment, apart from His constant care. You're never alone, never unloved. Your every tear is precious to Him; your every discovery of His goodness brings Him delight. He never tires of watching over you, guarding you night and day.

Dear sister, have you come to a place in your spiritual life where this describes your walk with God? Are you done with yourself and ready to honor God's great love for you by *truly loving Him in return*?

In response to this love, may your heart bow to Him more humbly, may His will joyfully become your own, may His Word be more desirous to you than your very next breath. Oh, that your every thought would be an outpouring of your gratitude to Him, that your every obedience, no matter the cost, become your love gift to Him.

May your Heavenly Father's love fill you so fully that nothing but His sweetness spills out of your life and onto those blessed to be near you.Notes

Notes

_____
_____
_____
_____
_____
_____
_____
_____
_____
_____
_____
_____
_____
_____
_____
_____
_____
_____
_____
_____
_____
_____
_____

Project Quiet Time

If you're serious about your spiritual transformation, (and I know you are!) then this project is non-negotiable! You see, we can't push up our sleeves and make change happen in our lives. We just don't have the power. We've already tried and failed so many times. The really good news is, God has all the power we need! Radical growth will come as we spend time alone with Him in His Word.

Talk over this page with God and make a plan to linger with Him.

When:_____

When will your daily date with God be? At the beginning of the day? After the kids get to school? Early while you can have a quiet house all to yourself? Will you split it into two or three sections like morning, noon and evening?

Where:_____

Where are you going to meet with God? Your favorite comfy chair, on the back porch, snuggled in bed...? Or do you need to create a special place?

What:_____

What are you going to do on your date with God? Plan what you will wear. You may need to lay out your big fuzzy robe and slippers. What will you do together? Will you talk, read, journal, ask, listen, think, plan, sing, study, dream or all of the above?

Why:_____

This may be the most important question to ponder. If you don't know the "why" of your daily time with God, it won't last past tomorrow. You'll let ridiculous excuses like, "I'm too busy" or "It's hard to get out of bed in the morning" come between you and your one True Love.

Heart Work

Day One
A Heart Consumed With God

Describe in detail the love relationship God desires to have with you.

- Ephesians 1:3-6

  _____
  _____
  _____

- Lamentations 4:2

  _____
  _____
  _____

- 1 John 4:9,10

  _____
  _____
  _____

- 1John 3:1

  _____
  _____
  _____

- Galatians 4:6

  _____
  _____
  _____

- Malachi 3:17

  _____
  _____
  _____

What one thing did God impress on my heart today?

Heart Work

Day Two
A Heart Consumed With God

Apply these verses to your life. What does God want you to *understand* or *do*?

- John 21:15

_____

_____

_____

- 1 Peter 1:7-8

_____

_____

_____

- Colossians 1:10

_____

_____

_____

- Titus 2:14

_____

_____

_____

_____

- Isaiah 62:5

_____

_____

_____

- Ephesians 5:25-32

_____

_____

_____

How can I make what I studied today a part of the rest of my life?

Heart Work

Day Three
A Heart Consumed With God

Take your time and carefully jot down what God says about your heart.

- Psalm 44:21

_____

_____

_____

- Proverbs 15:11

_____

_____

_____

- Luke 16:15

_____

_____

_____

- 1 Chronicles 28:9

_____

_____

_____

- Revelation 2:23

_____

_____

_____

What does God want to change in my life as a result of this study?

Heart-Work

Day Four
A Heart Consumed With God

In your own words explain what God knows from the following verses.

- Job 34:21

  _____

  _____

  _____

- Psalm 139:2,3

  _____

  _____

  _____

- Psalm 139:4

  _____

  _____

  _____

- 2 Samuel 7:20

  _____

  _____

  _____

- 2 Timothy 2:19

  _____

  _____

  _____

- Job 23:10

  _____

  _____

  _____

- Deuteronomy 2:7

  _____

  _____

  _____

- Matthew 6:8

  _____

  _____

  _____

- Exodus 3:7

  _____

  _____

  _____

- Matthew 10:29, 30

  _____

  _____

  _____

How do these truths bring me comfort?

Heart-Work

Day Five
A Heart Consumed With God

How does God want us to worship Him?

- 2 Samuel 7:22

  _____

  _____

  _____

- 2 Kings 19:15

  _____

  _____

  _____

- 1 Chronicles 17:20

  _____

  _____

  _____

- Psalm 86:10

  _____

  _____

  _____

- Isaiah 45:5-7

  _____

  _____

  _____

- Deuteronomy 32:3

  _____

  _____

  _____

Let me describe how I want to worship God after studying this...

Chapter Two

Priority Number One
A Heart Consumed With God

Heart-Verse

"Nevertheless I am continually with Thee;
Thou hast taken hold of my right hand.
With Thy counsel Thou wilt guide me,
and afterward receive me to glory.
Whom have I in heaven but Thee?
And besides Thee, I desire nothing on earth.
My flesh may fail, but God is the strength of my heart
and my portion forever.
For behold, those who are far from Thee will perish;
Thou hast destroyed all those who are unfaithful to Thee.
But as for me, the nearness of God is my good;
That I may tell of all Thy good works."

Psalm 73:23-28

Priority Number One
A Heart Consumed With God

My friend, you and I are on assignment by God! That's a lot to take in! The King of Kings and Lord of Lords has a dream, a plan for our life! I hope that excites you as much as it excites me!! Surely we don't want to miss out on a single blessing or opportunity to serve Him and bring Him glory, right?

I have a test question for you. When your thoughts have idle time between work and cooking and errands, where does your mind wander? Do your thoughts creep over to "If only …", or "I wish …", or "Why did it have to turn out like this…?" From time to time we all battle these dangerous thoughts.

Let me help save your sanity and your joy! Let's do what David did. Instead of letting our mind wander to all the things that worry, disappoint and hurt us… let's direct them to wander to all your blessings instead! Wouldn't that be brilliant and life-giving instead of joy-stealing!?

Let's start this new discipline with our thoughts and I promise our joy meter will be soaring! Meditating on the goodness of God will make us happier than chocolate. His sweetness to us is infinitely richer and lasts forever. From the minute we wake up in the morning until our last thought at night, let's train our brain to savor God's great love and tenderness for us.

Thinking God's thoughts may be a new discipline for you, especially if you're a negative person. Believe me, I know. The perfectionist in me is really good at being critical. Let's ask God for His help to turn our negative, worrisome thoughts into praise and gratitude. And here's the kicker, He'll help us! The more we spend time soaking up God's Word, the more He'll use it to change us from the inside out! God's Word is *the* agent of change. No amount of sheer willpower can bring the kind of change we need here. Change will come as we intentionally steer our thoughts to Him.

May Charles Spurgeon's words describe our new lives in Christ …

"Souls abiding in Jesus open the day with prayer, prayer surrounds them as an atmosphere all day long; at night they fall asleep praying."

Let's take a closer look at our key verses:

"Nevertheless I am continually with Thee;
Thou hast taken hold of my right hand.
With Thy counsel Thou wilt guide me, and afterward receive me to glory."

Not only will God never leave us, He's taken hold of our right hand so even if we want to wander off he'll hold us tight and keep giving us all the encouragement and guidance we'll ever need till the day comes when He finally brings us safely home to Him. It's like our whole Christian experience summed up in this one beautiful, simple verse. He'll hold us in this life and bring us safely to the next. No need to ever fear. He's simply got us!

"Whom have I in heaven but Thee?
And besides Thee, I desire nothing on earth.
My flesh may fail, but God is the strength of my heart and my portion forever."

We know He's the only One who's ever loved us perfectly! Every other love has failed us, hurt us, abandoned us. He really is the only One we have! He's our unfailing, constant strength and provider. If only we'd desire Him and only Him!

"For behold, those who are far from Thee will perish;
Thou hast destroyed all those who are unfaithful to Thee.
But as for me, the nearness of God is my good;
That I may tell of all Thy good works."

Oh, may His nearness be our sweetest blessing! May we never get over His love and desire for us! And no matter where we go or who we're with, may every conversation find us bragging on who He is and what He's done!

Lastly, may others be in awe of the love relationship we have with our Heavenly Father! And may they come to love Him too!

Project Evaluate

Are you enjoying God? What is your honest response? Have you really paused to consider *enjoying God* or has He been more of a duty or a relationship you always feel guilty about? Like, I *should* read my Bible, I *should* pray more, I *should* go to church more, I wonder of God's upset with me?

May I invite you to a fresh new start with God? The Bible is clear. He's waiting for you, longing for you. He's good at fresh starts and second chances. I know. I've had plenty!

Take some time to pause here and read Psalm 119 before you continue.

Am I enjoying God? 1 2 3 4 5 6 7 8 9 10
Circle one:

Please write your goals and the steps you're going to take to reach them.

My Goal
The kind of relationship I want with God is…

_____

_____

_____

_____

My Plan
My plan for an intimate closeness to God is…

_____

_____

_____

_____

Tell a friend about your new plan so she can pray with you!

Project Testimony

I know you'll eventually thank me for assigning you this project! It may be difficult if you've never done this before, and you may fill your trash can with lots of crumpled paper, but this may be one of the single most important projects in this 11-week course. As you share what the glorious gospel has done in your life, you have the potential to bring others to Christ as well!

Start by asking God for His help as you write the story of your salvation. I want you to write it in such a way that the gospel shines so brightly, a listener would be compelled to follow your footsteps and seek their own salvation from sin! In other words, the main character of your salvation story will be *Christ*, how *He* drew you, what *He* showed you, what *He* did on the cross for you. Many fall into the trap of talking too much about themselves as they share their testimony instead of Jesus, so just watch your use of the word "I".

My last writing tip is to remind you to add a few scriptures. Remember, it is *God's* Word that will not return void and it will be the tool God uses to pierce the hearts of your listeners.

May God bless you as you take time to ponder again the glorious path He brought you on to so great a salvation! May God use this project to give you boldness as you share your testimony with countless lost souls as well as encourage countless believers. After all, it is the greatest story ever told!

- Write an attention-getting beginning phrase.

- Be brief about a sordid past.

- Be specific about your need for forgiveness and Christ's finished work on the cross. Explain how sin separated you from a holy God. Explain sin.

- Try not to use terms such as, "born again, saved, redeemed, conversion" unless you take time to explain them. They may not understand that lingo. Try saying something like, "I was on my way to hell, but God made a way for me to go to heaven."

- Conclude with a description of how your whole life now shows your gratitude to Christ for all He did for you.

- Practice sharing your testimony over and over. Tell the waitress, your co-workers, teachers, and extended family. It'll be your very favorite story in all the world so tell it every single chance you get!

- Keep your final copy right here in your Makeover. Add a copy to your Bible, email one to family, friends, and me info@krisgoertzen.com! Post it on Facebook and in your scrapbooks, so you can be a testimony to future generations!

My Testimony

_____
_____
_____
_____
_____
_____
_____
_____
_____
_____
_____
_____
_____
_____
_____
_____
_____
_____

Heart-Work

Day Six
A Heart Consumed With God

Describe what must happen in order for you to enjoy God. Begin each sentence with, "I must…"

- Psalm 32:1-7

_____
_____
_____

- 2 Corinthians 5:17

_____
_____
_____

- 2 Timothy 3:16,17

_____
_____
_____

- Psalm 119:105

_____
_____
_____

- Psalm 119:24

_____
_____
_____

- Psalm 37:31

_____

_____

_____

- Romans 12:1, 2

_____

_____

_____

- Matthew 6:33

_____

_____

_____

- 1 Corinthians 6:20

_____

_____

_____

- Colossians 3:17

_____

_____

_____

- Romans 8:14

_____

_____

_____

Please summarize how this lesson changes your thinking/living?

Heart-Work

Day Seven
A Heart Consumed With God

What does God say is true of every Christian?

- John 3:16

_____

_____

_____

- Romans 6:8

_____

_____

_____

- Romans 6:14

_____

_____

_____

- Romans 8:37

_____

_____

_____

- 2 Corinthians 5:7

_____

_____

_____

- Ephesians 1:3

_____

_____

_____

- Ephesians 1:7

_____

_____

_____

- Philippians 4:13

_____

_____

_____

How does this encourage me?

Heart-Work

Day Eight
A Heart Consumed With God

What does God continue to say is true of every Christian?

- I John 5:4

_____

_____

- Psalm 32:1,2

_____

_____

- Isaiah 43:25

_____

_____

- Micah 7:19

_____

_____

- Ephesians 2:5-7

_____

_____

_____

- Ephesians 2:13,14

_____

_____

_____

- Ephesians 2:18-21

_____

_____

_____

- I Corinthians 6:19

_____

_____

_____

- Romans 8:16

_____

_____

_____

- Romans 8:26

_____

_____

_____

- 1 Peter 2:9,10

_____

_____

_____

- Revelation 1:5, 6

_____

_____

_____

How does this encourage and challenge me?

Heart-Work

Day Nine
A Heart Consumed With God

What is the chief purpose of every Christian?
- Mark 8:34-37

_____

_____

_____

What should be the chief purpose of every Christian?
- Matthew 6:33

_____

_____

- 1 Peter 4:11

_____

_____

_____

- 1 Corinthians 10:31

_____

_____

_____

- Colossians 3:17

_____

_____

_____

How can I live these truths every day?

Heart-Work

Day Ten
A Heart Consumed With God

How did Paul, a great man of God, describe himself?

- Romans 1:1

_____

_____

_____

- 1 Corinthians 1:1

_____

_____

_____

- Galatians1:10

_____

_____

_____

- Ephesians 4:1

_____

_____

_____

- 1 Timothy 1:15

_____

_____

_____

How should I describe myself?

Chapter Three

Priority Number Two
A Heart Prepared to serve

Heart-Verse

*"Do nothing from selfish or empty conceit,
But with humility of mind let each of you regard one another
As more important than himself;
Do not look out for your own personal interests,
But for the interests of others."*

Philippians 2:3

Priority Number Two
A Heart Prepared to Serve

We're going to spend the next two chapters, (really the rest of our lives!) making sure our hearts are responding rightly to God so we'll be prepared to serve others. The concept is that as we linger with Him daily, He fills our hearts to *overflowing*. It's that overflowing that will bless those near us. If our hearts aren't continually consumed with enjoying God, in daily study, meditation and prayer, we'll be dry, empty and crabby. Without God's continually filling, only ugliness will spill out of us!

I see us as sanctified colanders that are empty if we don't keep them under a constant flow, letting the water of the Word continually fill us and wash us.

But here's the problem, there are so many sins that lurk and hide in our hearts! Remember that verse in Jeremiah 17:9? Does it say something about our heart, being deceitful and desperately wicked? Our hearts always deceive us and want to fool us into thinking that we're just fine, that it's okay to be mediocre. During a recent sermon, my husband exhorted our precious congregation with these words…

> *"We plan our lives around the world and not around God,*
> *and wonder why our lives are mediocre."*

That can no longer be true of us! We can't be casual about God. We can't settle for lukewarm when God deserves so much more! Rather, let's say with the great George Whitefield,

> *"I pray to God this day to make me an extraordinary Christian."*

Imagine what might happen if we made that our waking prayer for the rest of our lives!

Next, let's take a look at what Paul has to say to us..."*Do nothing from selfish or empty conceit,*"

I remember how very clear Rick and I had to be when we'd instruct our children because one of them had an innate ability to find loopholes that served her purposes instead of ours. She loved to find as much wiggle room in the rules as she possibly could! And may I say, the apple didn't fall far from the tree! I've earned expert status at justifying things to meet my own goals and ambitions!

Paul doesn't give us *any* wiggle room in this verse! We are never, ever to be selfish. We are never, ever to think of our needs or preferences. We aren't even allowed to day-dream of what it would be like if we were to get our own way. "Do nothing from selfish or empty conceit. " Instead…

> *"But with humility of mind let each of you regard one another*
> *As more important than himself;*
> *Do not look out for your own personal interests,*
> *But for the interests of others."*

Since *all* my needs are met in the Lord, since He holds me by the hand and guides me and fills me with His choicest blessings, it's easy to put myself on the back burner. (Or it should be!) Since God's got me, and has filled me to overflowing, I can put the needs of others first! I can truly lift my eyes off myself and have Jesus's eyes to see the needs around me and work hard to meet them as if I were serving Jesus, Himself!

Notice it's a mindset. My thoughts must be constantly putting others first, dreaming of ways to bless them, surprise them, honor them, appreciate them, taking no thought for myself. I'm not worried about equal treatment. I'm not waiting for my turn to be appreciated. It's not going to be easy, but, oh, the blessings that will come when we crave being a blessing to others for Jesus!

May God use this lesson to challenge us to His higher calling. Let's invite Him start working on our hearts so He can use us like crazy for His glory. Just imagine! The High King of Heaven wants to use you! We could never come up with a more honorable or exciting calling than God using us.

I'll never forget the day my mother brought a poverty stricken old woman into our home. Her husband was to have a surgical procedure so my mom volunteered to care for her.

As a young junior high girl, I didn't look for this woman's heart, instead I shamefully only noticed the outward. She had grey stringy hair, deep crevices in her face with bit of a beard and she didn't smell very good...at all.

These were all shocking to me. But it was what I watched my mom do that day, that has stayed with me my whole life. She treated this woman with dignity and kindness. That day my mom gave her whole life to that woman. She didn't just serve her, she anticipated her every need. That poor woman was bound to a wheelchair so my mom even helped her in the bathroom. The whole day made me quite uncomfortable.

Looking back, it's my first memory of anyone selflessly serving someone in need as Jesus would. At the time, I didn't know Jesus, but now I see what my mom did that day as breathtakingly beautiful. She didn't get any recognition, no one at church gave her a round of applause or admired her from the pulpit. But Jesus was watching and I hope He felt my mother's deep love for Him. And a little junior high girl was watching and she was marked forever.

I hope you're ready to do some honest sin-hunting so we too can be selfless servers. We aren't going to pretend anymore that there isn't sin and selfishness lingering in our hearts. We're going to choose right here, right now, not to excuse our lazy habits, lousy excuses and our disregard for others. We're going to get rid of those things and confess them so we can be ready for a life of unequaled excitement being used by God Himself to be a blessing to others!

Let's take a moment and ask the Holy Spirit for His courage to search our hearts and motives...I have a feeling we are going to need it!

Heavenly Father,

Please show me what lurks in my heart that hinders my use to You. I know that many times I make excuses for my sin; I try to justify it and try to hide it. I don't want to do that anymore because it ruins my ability to reflect You.
Help me to live for You.
I cant do it without Your help.
I love You.

Amen

Notes

_____
_____
_____
_____
_____
_____
_____
_____
_____
_____
_____
_____
_____
_____
_____
_____
_____
_____
_____
_____
_____
_____
_____
_____

Project schedule

"The plans of the diligent lead surely to advantage,
But everyone who is hasty comes surely to poverty."
Proverbs 21:5

Here's my paraphrase…

She who schedules her days will be blessed with elegance and order,
but she who flies by the seat of her pants will scare others
and have a nervous breakdown by supper.

Every night before you turn out the light on your bed-side table, I want to invite you to end your day with me. I'm usually propped up with pillows, snuggled in my blankets with my Bible, a pen, my date book, paper, and one or two of the books I am reading. I try to end each day as I began it, with the Lord. Before I drop into weary unconsciousness, I take a piece of paper and my date book and begin to pray over the day ahead. First, I fold my paper in half from top to bottom. Then, I write out my priorities on the left side, just as Elizabeth George taught me to do years ago. With "God" at the top of my list, I thoughtfully ask the Lord how I can show Him how much I love Him in the day ahead. I linger there until the Holy Spirit impresses something on my heart. Maybe I need to spend more time thinking about Him, Maybe I need to have a more grateful heart, maybe I need to share Him more, maybe there's a verse I need to meditate on. I write that down under "God" on my priority list.

Under that, I write "My Heart." Again, I ask the Lord to show me if there's anything that's lingering in my heart that hinders me from serving Him completely. Maybe I've been grouchy, negative, selfish…goodness; the list could go on and on! After I confess it, I prayerfully write down something proactive I can do to keep my colander clean and my heart ready to serve. Maybe I need to read a book to help me in a certain area, or seek counsel from a godly friend, or apply a memorized verse, or discipline my thoughts, or ask for accountability. I continue the same way with each priority.

If each day is a gift from God, are we not obligated to seek Him as how to spend it? Do we forget that the same God who created the universe also has plans and purposes for us? Time is a precious, precious gift that I can choose to squander or use for the glory of God. Since I desperately want my life to count for God, then my days, hours and minutes must be used with care and precision.

I want to share some of my favorite quotes; most are written in the back of my Bible. They inspire me to use my time wisely for the Lord and help hold me accountable. I hope these quotes inspire you too! Mediate on them often!

"We must say no, not only to things which are wrong and sinful,
but to things that are pleasant and good,
which would hinder and clog our grand duties and our chief work."
C.A. Stoddards

"The Christian life does not grow by accident."
Dr. Rick Goertzen

"Sin leads us to take short-cuts in all Christian disciplines."
John MacArthur

"...at the heart of the disciplined spiritual life is the discipline of time."
Donald S. Whitney

"You are going to be what you are now becoming."
Dawson Trotman

"Attack this life, live for God, because Heaven's waiting."
Dr. Rick Goertzen

"God's glory is more important than my schedule."
Donna Morely

Please use the following format to schedule your day. It'll take a couple weeks, but I promise you'll be more productive and feel good about it too…after all, happiness is a checked off to-do list, right? As Proverbs says, "Desire realized is sweet to the soul." I get so excited about accomplishing things throughout the day…that if I do something that isn't on my to-do list, I write it in just so I can check it off! Do you do that too!?

But mostly, this format will be a daily reminder of God's priorities for you!

My Priorities

God

"Dear God, how can I live tomorrow to show that You are everything to me?"

My Heart

"Dear God, is there anything hindering my love and service for you?"

My Husband

"Dear God, how can I spoil and honor my husband with love today?"

My Children

"Dear God, how can I lavish each of my children with love today?"

Others

"Dear God, who can You use me to be a blessing to today?"

My Schedule

Wake time:

Time with God:

My Heart:

My Husband:

Each Child:

Others:

Planning Time:
Lights Out:

Heart-Work

Day One
A Heart Prepared to Serve

To prepare our hearts to serve, let's find out how God feels about pride.

- Proverbs 21:4

_____
_____
_____

- Proverbs 16:5

_____
_____
_____

- Proverbs 16:18

_____
_____
_____

- Proverbs 8:13

_____
_____
_____

- James 4:6

_____
_____
_____

- Isaiah 13:11

_____
_____
_____

Do I hate my pride as much as God does or do I even notice it

Day Two
A Heart Prepared to Serve

What else does God want you to understand about pride?

- Matthew 23:12

_____

_____

- Proverbs 13:10

_____

_____

- Proverbs 18:12

_____

_____

- Mark 7:21-23

_____

_____

- 1 Samuel 2:3

_____

_____

Where does pride lurk in my heart?

Heart-Work

Day Three
A Heart Prepared to Serve

Describe Jesus' beautiful example of humility.

- Matthew 11:29

_____

_____

_____

- John 13:14-15

_____

_____

_____

- Philippians 2:5-8

_____

_____

_____

After thinking about these verses, please explain them in your own words.

- Micah 6:8

_____

_____

_____

- Psalm 138:6

_____

_____

_____

How can I begin to live more humbly like Jesus?

Heart-Work

Day Four
A Heart Prepared to Serve

What does God want me to learn from each of these verses?
- Matthew 11:29

_____
_____
_____

- Isaiah 66:2

_____
_____
_____

- Psalm 9:12

_____
_____
_____

- Matthew 20:26-28

_____
_____
_____

- Colossians 3:12

_____
_____
_____

How can I live what I have learned today?

Heart-Work

Day Five
A Heart Prepared to Serve

What is God telling me in each of the following verses?
- 1 Peter 1:17

_____

_____

_____

- Ephesians 5:16

_____

_____

_____

- Colossians 4:5

_____

_____

_____

- Acts 17:26

_____

_____

_____

- Ecclesiastes 3:1-8

_____

_____

_____

How can I make the most of this day for God?

Chapter Four

Priority Number Two
A Heart Prepared to Serve

Heart-Verse

"I will go before you and make the rough places smooth;
I will shatter the doors of bronze, and cut through their iron bars.
And I will give you the treasures of darkness,
And hidden wealth of secret places,
In order that you might know it is I, the LORD, the God of Israel,
who calls you by name."

Isaiah 45:2, 3

Priority Number Two
A Heart Prepared to Serve

How often do you wish for a 34-hour day? Certainly those extra 10 hours would allow you to finish the trail of unfinished tasks that drag behind you, right? You'd be able to lay your head on your pillow at night with a sense of peace and accomplishment for a day well done. But, truth be told, in the back of your mind you know that you'd clutter up those 10 hours like all the rest and be just as frustrated as you are right now.

We need relief from the ocean of unfinished letters, unfinished business, unread books, unvisited friends. "A mother's work is never done"? Well, neither is a homemaker's, a teacher's, a nurse's, a student's, a business woman's, or a Sunday school teacher's. We keep hoping that around the next corner we'll find time to catch up. Instead of finding more time, we find more tasks. So we work harder and enjoy life less. It can feel like sand slipping through our fingers.

Then we can find ourselves in a constant battle against guilt as we try to juggle it all, nurture our families, keep a beautiful home, time in the Word, care for ourselves, friends, job, school, extended family… We can end up feeling devoured with nothing left to give.

But here's the thing. It's not a problem of enough time, but of priorities. We can't let the urgent crowd out the important or the temporary rob the timeless.

Understand this, dear friends, *the need is not the call*. We can't meet *all* the needs presented to us. We aren't supposed to and we have to come to grips with that fact. I remember Elisabeth Elliott saying, "Not only does God love me and have a wonderful plan for my life…everyone loves me and has a plan for my life!" We can't succumb to all the needs presented to us by well meaning friends. We have to carefully discern our priorities in 24 hour increments.

God, who made us with limitations won't be the One who fills our schedules and weighs us down until we have stomach disorders, heart attacks and nervous breakdowns. Let's learn the differences between the constant demand of others and God's perfect will for us. We might need to jettison a few things from our calendar so we don't miss what has eternal significance.

Let's trust our key verse! God indeed goes before us and prepares the way… whether the way ahead has diapers or errands or counseling a friend through a tragedy. He'll work it all out in such a way that we'll be in awe of Him and burst into worship for the incredible things He has done!

It's my dream that we'll be able to say like Jesus in John 17:4 when He came to the end of HIs life, "I finished the work which Thou gavest me to do."

Psalm 103:13, 14
"Just as a father has compassion on his children,
So the LORD has compassion on those who fear Him.
For He knows our frame;
He is mindful that we are dust."

God's great servant Nehemiah prayed and planned. The two went hand in hand as he carried the heavy burden of concern for his people who were living in ruin. Nehemiah's praying and planning prepared him for the tremendous work God had for him. When the King asked Nehemiah, he was ready, prepared, focused, not whining about all he had to do. He would have failed if he had not planned ahead while he prayed. What a great lesson for us!

If you fail to plan you plan to fail.

That sounds very simplistic, doesn't it? It's simple, but it's true. Think back to the last time you were running late with your hair on fire and all the yelling and drama that went with it. For me, 99.9% of the time it's because I'm the one who didn't plan well. The fault lies with me. I need to plan ahead!

I can make idols of my plans without even knowing it. Have you ever done that? This prayer is a tremendous help to keep my heart in the right place. Please pray this with me often…
"Lord, I give up all my own plans and purposes,
All my own desires and hopes and accept Thy will for my life.
I give myself, my life, my all, utterly to Thee forever.
Fill me with Thy Holy Spirit,
Use me where Thou wilt, send me where Thou wilt,
Work out Thy whole will in my life at any cost
Now and forever."
Betty Stam

My Favorite Time Management Tips

- Make a daily schedule and to-do list the night before, pray over it.
- Begin each day in prayer.
- Plan dinner the night before.
- Discover the crock pot.
- Limit phone calls, do light house work while on phone.
- Practice saying "no" in the mirror.
- Delegate.
- Schedule extended time away with God for prayer and planning.
- Keep your commitments.
- Recover lost items with prayer.
- Organize errands to one day out per week.
- Be at the grocery store no more than once per week.
- Plan ahead to go at slow hours.
- Entertain simply.
- Eliminate and concentrate.
- Give each task a time limit.
- Bring projects to work on in waiting rooms and on road trips.
- Be content with what you have.
- Go to bed early, without your phone.
- Resist the urge to read junk mail.
- Be best friends with your trash can.
- Be selective in your reading, read deep challenging books.
- Limit wardrobe to just a handful of favorite pieces, give the rest away.
- Mark in your books for future reference.
- Exercise daily for increased energy and better sleep.
- Pray for success and bargains when you shop.
- Repeat this mantra: Do it, do it right, do it right now.
- Ask for help in areas you are weak, i.e. organizing, menus, finances.
- Kill clutter.
- Take a good vitamin.
- Race the clock when cleaning house.

Project Ponder

Please come here often to ponder these quotes. Let them stir your heart.

"My selfishness mars my exaltation of Christ." Dr. Rick Goertzen

"Great abilities don't make you useful to God."
Elizabeth Inrig

"All sin is found in secret atheism…
Every sin is a kind of cursing God in the heart,
An aim at the destruction of the being of God, not actually, but virtually…
A man in every sin aims to set up his own rule,
And his own glory at the end of his actions."
Stephen Charnock

"You will never deny yourself if you don't think Christ is worth it."

"A humble man has lower thoughts of himself than others have of him."

"My greatest fear is to be a nominal Christian."

"I am convinced there is nothing more beautiful than a woman whose heart belongs to God."

"Christ Jesus came into the world to save sinners-of whom I am the worst." 1 Timothy 1:15

"There is absolutely nothing lost in self-denial. " Dr. Rick Goertzen

"Be not angry that you cannot make others as you wish them to be, since you cannot make yourself as you wish yourself to be."
Thomas A Kempis

Project Evaluate

Can you answer these questions with confidence?

Why am I here?
I am on assignment by God to...

_____

_____

_____

Have I been a casual Christian? Yes __ No__

Explain your answer...

_____

_____

_____

What am I going to do about it?

_____

_____

_____

What is hindering my spiritual growth?

_____

_____

_____

What am I going to do about it?

_____

_____

_____

Heart-Work

Day Six
A Heart Prepared to Serve

What is God telling you about your planning and time management?

- 1 Corinthians 14:40

_____

_____

_____

- Job 5:8-12, especially verse 12

_____

_____

_____

- Proverbs 16:3

_____

_____

_____

- Proverbs 16:9

_____

_____

_____

- Proverbs 4:26

_____

_____

_____

- Proverbs 20:18

_____

_____

_____

- Proverbs 21:5

_____

_____

_____

- Ephesians 5:15-17

_____

_____

_____

- Luke 14:28-30

_____

_____

_____

- Jeremiah 29:11

_____

_____

_____

- Mark 1:2-3

_____

_____

_____

How can I best glorify God with my time?

Heart-Work

Day Seven
A Heart Prepared to Serve

What is God specifically asking me to understand about my tongue?

- Psalm 141:3

_____

_____

_____

- Proverbs 12:18

_____

_____

_____

- Proverbs 12:25

_____

_____

_____

- Proverbs 14:7

_____

_____

_____

- Proverbs 15:1

_____

_____

_____

- Proverbs 15:4

_____

_____

- Proverbs 15:23

_____

_____

- Proverbs 15:28

_____

_____

- Proverbs 16:13

_____

_____

- Proverbs 16:21

_____

_____

- Proverbs 16:23

_____

_____

- Proverbs 16:24

_____

_____

_____

Pray for strength so you can obey God in these areas.

Heart-Work

Day Eight
A Heart Prepared to Serve

What is God specifically instructing me to do in these verses?

- Proverbs 17:27

_____

_____

_____

- Proverbs 17:28

_____

_____

_____

- Proverbs 18:8

_____

_____

_____

- Proverbs 20:19

_____

_____

_____

- Proverbs 21:23

_____

_____

_____

- Proverbs 22:11

_____

_____

- Proverbs 25:11

_____

_____

- Proverbs 25:15

_____

_____

- Proverbs 25:20

_____

_____

- Proverbs 29:20

_____

_____

- Proverbs 30:32

_____

_____

- Proverbs 31:26

_____

_____

Ask God to change your heart so your words will be beautiful for Him.

Heart-Work

Day Nine
A Heart Prepared to Serve

What plan does God have for me? Notice the key word.

- Leviticus 11:45

_____
_____
_____

- Romans 12:1

_____
_____
_____

- 1 Peter 1:15,16

_____
_____
_____

- Hebrews 12:14

_____
_____
_____

- Ephesians 1:4

_____
_____
_____

- 2 Timothy 1:9

_____

_____

_____

- Luke 1:74-75

_____

_____

_____

- 2 Peter 3:8-11

_____

_____

_____

- 1 Thessalonians 3:11-13

_____

_____

_____

- 1 Chronicles 16:29

_____

_____

_____

Stop and thank God now for His perfection and holiness.

Heart-Work

Day Ten
A Heart Prepared to Serve

What does God's love demand of me? Notice the key word.

- Deuteronomy 13:4

_____

_____

_____

- Exodus 19:5

_____

_____

_____

- Jeremiah 7:23

_____

_____

_____

- 2 Corinthians 10:5

_____

_____

_____

- Romans 6:17

_____

_____

_____

- 1 Samuel 15:22

_____

_____

_____

- Philippians 2:5-8

_____

_____

_____

- Hebrews 5:8

_____

_____

_____

- Jeremiah 38:20

_____

_____

_____

- Psalm 18:44a

_____

_____

_____

Ask the Holy Spirit to give you His power to obey.

Chapter Five

Priority Number Three
A Heart Devoted to My Husband

Heart-Verse

"An excellent wife, who can find?
The heart of her husband trusts in her,
And he will have no lack of gain.
She does him good and not evil all the days of her life."

Proverbs 31:10-12

Priority Number Three
A Heart Devoted to My Husband

If you're like me, your marriage isn't what you dreamed it would be. Now, after 34 years I can bless God that He didn't let it live up to my shallow expectations. But back in the day I sure struggled! I walked down that isle with all the wrong expectations. It was as if I tossed the vibrant relationship I had with the Lord out the window and expected Rick to take the place of God in my life.

I thought my expectations would serve us well. I'd be Sleeping Beauty while Rick would be Prince Charming. I thought if he'd always treat me like a princess our marriage would be a real-life fairytale of fulfillment and bliss. I'm embarrassed now at how very selfish my expectations were! Instead of dreaming of ways to serve my wonderful husband, I was dreaming of ways he could serve and worship me. You can imagine how crushed and disillusioned I became when I finally realized I wasn't going to be his idol.

While there have been fairy tale moments, there's been a far more magical lesson I learned along the way. (Poor Rick, he probably wonders why I always have to learn God's lessons the hard way!) I learned that my expectations were wrong. First, I expected him to be perfect according to *my* standards. I didn't give him room to figure things out or to make mistakes. I had to point out all his shortcomings and correct them. Second, without realizing it in the moment, I expected his life to revolve around me and not the Lord. What I had found most attractive when we were dating was his whole-hearted pursuit of serving God as a pastor. How horrid that I wanted to distract him from that! Third, I didn't expect to have to apply 1 Corinthians 13, to deny self, or that I'd have trials in my marriage. I thought it would be easy. And maybe it would have been easier if I hadn't been such a mess!

In His goodness, God denied my dream of a fairy tale marriage and instead used it as a sometimes painful tool to show me areas of my life that were full of selfishness. Nothing's more miserable than when God shows me it's time for another ugly behavior to be ripped out of my life. But, I'm so glad He loves me enough to weed out my sin! I hope little by little through this sanctification process, I'm reflecting more of Christ to God's eyes … and to Rick's!

Today I feel more fulfilled than ever because I'm focusing on how God lavishes me with His blessings. I feel loved because *God* loves me beyond my imagination. And you know Rick's thrilled to be off the hook, no longer responsible for my happiness! Once I got that settled and realized my role in our marriage, everything changed! There's the wonderful joy of friendship now and mutual ministry to each other. I literally couldn't ask for more!

I had our theme verse for this chapter in mind when I wrote my wedding vows. I earnestly promised Rick I'd do him good and not evil all the days of my life. But I realize haven't lived up to those vows and that's why it's so important to me to get this Bible study in the hands and hearts of as many women as I can. I want to save other women from the heartache that I had, and caused, because I just didn't know better. I needed another woman to come alongside me and help me. I want to be that friend to you!

As I am writing this, my husband called to tell me a dear man in our church family died unexpectedly. I'm broken-hearted for his precious wife whose husband is suddenly gone from her. I wonder if in her pain and loss, her advice to us would be to hold our husbands tightly and let all the rest go. That's exactly what we need to do, love our husbands like there's no tomorrow.

As I write this, I'm begging you not to make the same mistakes I made. Please enjoy your husband and the differences between you. And when those differences bring conflict, instead of demanding that *he* change, hurry into God's presence to ask if it's something *you* can change. Pray for a painful reluctance to point out his shortcomings. Try to ignore them while you give them to God in prayer. And above all, don't withhold love. Don't let him feel rejection from you when he doesn't measure up to your expectations. Where would we be if God treated us that way?

Notes

_____
_____
_____
_____
_____
_____
_____
_____
_____
_____
_____
_____
_____
_____
_____
_____
_____
_____
_____
_____
_____
_____

Project Change

If you're like me, you believe in doing everything with as much excellence as you can muster. Ideally, I want to do things with excellence for Christ, but honestly sometimes I want to do things with excellence because it feeds my pride. Even worse, I want my dear husband to make certain changes so he can live up to *my* version of excellence. Isn't that terrible? I'm sure you can't relate.

When it comes to change, I have a principle that protects my precious husband from all my best intentions. I used to work hard to change him. Even though he was the most marvelous man I'd ever known, I still saw tiny little improvements that were sure to help him be even more useful for the kingdom. Yes, I was *that arrogant* to think I could help the Holy Spirit mold him to be more like Christ. Ugh, ugh, ugh! God had to peel my fingers off my husband and show me that he wasn't my job. My job was to work on the log in my own eye. Sigh! Life is so much sweeter as I try to focus on changing *me* not him. Rick's off limits. He's in God's hands, not mine. I pray for him…but I work on changing *me*.

This brings me to a very important question for you and you alone. You're not allowed to ask your husband for his input. You need to be prayerful, sensitive and observant as you ponder your answer. *In a month or two* you can ask your husband for his input, but for now I want to train you to ask yourself this question often.

What's the one area of my life that my husband would like me to work on?

Please record your answer here:

_____

_____

_____

Why do I need to work on this?

_____

_____

_____

_____

_____

_____

What's my plan to change?

_____

_____

_____

_____

_____

_____

Write a prayer asking for God's help.

_____

_____

_____

_____

_____

_____

Project Negative

One of the most common problems women share with me is their desire to break free of the negativity that seems to rule their lives. It often becomes such a deep rut that they don't know how to break free. This list will offer you dramatic help! Let me warn you though, you'll feel the Holy Spirit convict you and that's a good thing! So ask God for strength, not only to face this list honestly, but to root these things out of your life once and for all! If you're like me you'll be asking for His forgiveness and help over and over.

Now here's the kicker! I want you to prayerfully read this list through every single day this week. If you're serious about being Christlike and bringing joy to your husband you'll do it. Also, reading this every day will better prepare you for next week's list!

Keys to a Truly Miserable Marriage

1. Second guess his decisions.
2. Complain about everything.
3. Have expectations he can never meet.
4. Hint instead of communicate.
5. Belittle his ideas.
6. Argue in front of the children.
7. Raise your voice.
8. Finish his sentences.
9. Bring up past failures.
10. Run up your credit card balance.
11. Be moody.
12. Give him the silent treatment.
13. Wish for the good old days.
14. Jump to conclusions.
15. Accuse him.
16. Criticize his attempts to please you.
17. Always see the negative.
18. Seek revenge.
19. Make him late.
20. Interrupt him.
21. Be disinterested in love-making.

22. Make fun of him in public.
23. Withhold your approval.
24. Correct him in front of others.
25. Gripe about his hobbies.
26. Compare him to other men.
27. Nit-pick.
28. Be apathetic about his concerns.
29. Drift from God.
30. Be depressed.
31. Complain about his family.
32. Ignore him.
33. Be jealous.
34. Preach at him.
35. Violate his trust.
36. Set him up to fail.
37. Neglect yourself.
38. Doubt his motives.
39. Try to be his conscience.
40. Resent his income level.
41. Demand your own way.
42. Reject his efforts to show his love for you.
43. Never admit when you are wrong.
44. Fail to keep your word.
45. Tell him you should never have gotten married.
46. Make mountains out of molehills.
47. Always think the worst.
48. Over commit.
49. Take everything personally.
50. Insist on having the last word.

If God has opened your eyes and you are under conviction in some of these areas, please go to your husband and ask him to forgive you. Ask him to be patient with you while you seek to change and to pray with you for God's help. God will reward your obedience and humble heart in dramatic ways! Remember our verse from chapter one? *"But to this one will I look, To him who is humble and contrite of spirit, and who trembles at My Word."*

Heart-Work

Day One
A Heart Devoted to My Husband

Describe the kind of wife God is telling you to be in His wisdom book.

- Proverbs 5:18,19

_____

_____

_____

- Proverbs 12:4

_____

_____

_____

- Proverbs 18:22

_____

_____

_____

- Proverbs 19:13

_____

_____

_____

- Proverbs 21:9

_____

_____

_____

- Proverbs 21:19

_____

_____

_____

- Proverbs 27:15

_____

_____

_____

_____

- Proverbs 31:10

_____

_____

_____

What is the one thing God is asking me to apply from today's study?

Heart-Work

Day Two
A Heart Devoted to My Husband

As you summarize each verse, please notice the theme of today's assignment.

- Romans 15:3

_____
_____
_____

- Philippians 2:21

_____
_____
_____

- 2 Corinthians 5:15

_____
_____
_____

- 1 Corinthians 10:24

_____
_____
_____

- 1 Corinthians 13:5b

_____
_____
_____

- 1 Corinthians 10:33

_____

_____

_____

- 2 Timothy 3:2a

_____

_____

_____

In your prayer time today, ask God to help you make a new commitment to be selfless like Jesus so your life will have a beautiful focus on God and others instead of yourself.

Heart-Work

Day Three
A Heart Devoted to My Husband

Please note the actions God tells us to take as wives.

- Genesis 2:18

_____

_____

_____

- Genesis 2:24

_____

_____

_____

- 1 Corinthians 7:2

_____

_____

_____

- Titus 2:4

_____

_____

_____

- Ephesians 5:33

_____

_____

_____

- 1 Corinthians 7:3

_____

_____

_____

- 1 Corinthians 7:10

_____

_____

_____

- Proverbs 31:12

_____

_____

_____

**What action is the Holy Spirit prompting you to take
toward your husband today?**

Heart-Work

Day Four
A Heart Devoted to My Husband

What sinful behavior can you to learn avoid from these wives of old? You may need to read some surrounding verses to understand the context.

- Judges 14:15-17

_____

_____

_____

- 2 Samuel 6:16

_____

_____

_____

- 1 Kings 21:25

_____

_____

_____

- Esther 5:14

_____

_____

_____

- Job 2:9

_____

_____

_____

- Acts 5:1, 2

_____

_____

_____

Please take time to confess to the Lord any similar behaviors you have had from today's lesson. Please also ask for your husband's forgiveness.

Heart-Work

Day Five
A Heart Devoted to My Husband

We often put our trust in our husbands. Where does God ask us to put our trust? Why?

- Nahum 1:7

_____
_____
_____

- Psalm 36:7

_____
_____
_____

- Psalm 9:10

_____
_____
_____

- Proverbs 3:5

_____
_____
_____

- Psalm 71:5

_____
_____
_____

- Psalm 13:5

_____

_____

_____

- Psalm 119:42

_____

_____

_____

- 2 Samuel 22:3

_____

_____

_____

- Psalm 56:11

_____

_____

_____

How can I make my trust in God obvious today?

Chapter Six

Priority Number Three
A Heart Devoted to My Husband

Heart-Verse

"Now therefore, I pray Thee,
Teach me Thy ways, that I may know Thee,
So I may find favor in Thy sight."

Exodus 33:13

Priority Number Three
A Heart Devoted to My Husband

Just recently, I asked my husband what he liked best about marriage. I loved what he said, "companionship." His answer made me stop and reflect on how destructive my best intentions were when we first got married. I thought if I worked hard enough I could ensure a happy marriage. So many times I had gotten out my magnifying glass and was looking for any tell-tale sign of impending doom. Nothing escaped my inspection. I easily cast aside his pleas for me to just relax and enjoy our relationship. How could I possibly relax when I was on assignment by God to protect and improve this marriage? As you're probably already guessing, I made us both miserable. On a regular basis I corrected, fixed, complained, manipulated, over-reacted and assumed the worst. The more my tactics for a happy marriage back-fired, the more determined I became to control our marriage.

I remember one day Rick did something silly hoping I would laugh. But I couldn't laugh. I was too grouchy and burdened that some evil was going to slip in and destroy us and too irritated that Rick could just breeze through life and not be on the lookout with me. The words I heard him say softly under his breath ripped through my heart, "you're just not the girl I married." Wow. God deeply humbled me at that very moment. Suddenly God showed me He didn't need me. It came as quite a shock. Rick had been right all along. I needed to stop worrying and trying to do God's job and just enjoy the process. That's when the fun in our marriage began!

God taught me some precious lessons.

#1 I was to focus on loving, not fixing, my husband.

#2 God wanted me to listen and obey the man He gave me.

I dedicated myself and my marriage to God all over again, this time with a promise not to interfere. I would leave Rick alone so he could hear the Holy Spirit instead of my constant nagging. And to my great surprise, our marriage became so incredible! With God in His rightful place, my expectations became realistic, my over-reacting ceased, there was no need to manipulate and God showed me that if I complained…it was really against HIM that I was complaining. Needless to say, complaining didn't seem like a good idea anymore. My new, biblical outlook freed me to do what God wants every wife to do, just love their husband like crazy!

After decades of marriage, I'm happy to report that God has never once disappointed me. Besides being madly in love, Rick and I are best friends. We can't wait to spend time together sharing, laughing, and loving every day.

Are there bumps along the way? You know there are bumps. It's funny though, how they seem to be noticeable only when my sinful heart rears it's ugly head. *I have to spend time making sure my heart is happy in God.* If I don't, well sure enough, the demanding, complaining and all the rest come roaring back.

These days I work to stay focused on my own heart before God. There seems to be plenty there to keep me busy. When I'm consumed with my closeness to God, I stop demanding so much of my poor husband. You too?

It's been a glorious lesson to learn in my marriage that my ways are not His ways. His are always, always best. I often need to pray as Moses did, *"teach me Thy ways, that I may know Thee, so I may find favor in Thy sight."* His ways, not mine.

How about you? Are you happy in God? Are you focusing your own heart on God? Are you consumed with your closeness to Him? Please let my encouragement reach your heart. Please focus on your growth, not your husband's. Don't make an idol out of what you want your marriage to be. Don't whine if your husband doesn't pray with you. Don't belittle him if he doesn't have family devotions or go to church every time the doors are open. Remember for now, "It is what it is"…and let God do the rest. Your part is to love him like crazy and let God astound you with His goodness, *in His time*. And pray with me, *"teach me Thy ways, that I may know Thee, So I may find favor in Thy sight."* Exodus 33:13

Project Positive

Okay, girls, here's the list you've been waiting for! Now that you've successfully rooted out *all* the negative in your life, you can replace it with these wonderful blessings! I want you to plow through this list and make these blessings new habits in your everyday life. That means you'll have to review this list every hour on the hour. Okay, how about at least every morning and evening for a month or so? Then you can try just a couple times a week and see how you do. The problem is, we are forgetters. Like the apostle Paul, the good we want to do, we forget to do, because we revert to getting caught up in ourselves again. This list will help set us free from our selfish habits and remind us we are on assignment by God to bless our husbands...so let's get to it!

One day Rick saw this list that I carry around with me. He took a yellow highlighter and marked the ones that were important to him and left it on the coffee table where he found it. I was so thrilled when I read what meant love to him! You may ask your husband to get out his highlighter in about a month or so, *after* you have made all these blessings a <u>habit</u> in your life.

Keys to a Truly Marvelous Marriage

1. Make eyes at him from across the room.
2. Every morning ask him "What can I do for you today?"
3. Respond to him with, "Sure, honey! I'd love to!"
4. Have a contented heart.
5. Send him to work with a steamy love letter.
6. Choose to be predictably happy every day.
7. Show genuine interest in his job/hobbies.
8. Ask his advise...and take it!
9. Meet him at the door after work with a huge welcome home hug.
10. Initiate love-making.
11. Laugh a lot.
12. Make a huge fuss over his attempts to please you.
13. Consistently have dinner ready at his preferred time.
14. Look your very best for him every day.
15. Praise him in public.
16. Correspond with his family.
17. Offer a back rub.
18. Kiss him passionately.

19. Keep his clothes laundered and pressed.
20. Share with him what God is doing in your life.
21. Stay within your budget no matter what.
22. Hold his hand often.
23. Plan a romantic evening at home without the children.
24. Thank him continually for providing for you.
25. Quickly admit you were wrong.
26. Enjoy watching his favorite show with him.
27. Show him something you want him to do during love-making.
28. Surprise him with little gifts.
29. Follow through with his wishes even when he's not present.
30. Buy some pretty new under clothes.
31. Choose a soft, sweet tone of voice.
32. Play footsie with him under the table.
33. Instill God's Word in your children's lives.
34. Tell him often how glad you are that God chose him for you.
35. Offer to help him with a project.
36. Encourage his dreams.
37. Use a masculine pet name for him.
38. Stay abreast and conversational about current events.
39. Send him thank you notes in the mail.
40. Ask him to share something he would like you to work on.
41. Tell the children all the reasons you love their Daddy.
42. Ask him to pray about something for you.
43. Keep your walk with God vibrant.
44. Choose to spend time with him over others.
45. Ask his permission before volunteering.
46. Make him laugh often.
47. Tell him how much you miss him when you are apart.
48. Support him completely in front of the children.
49. Be a good listener.
50. Ask him how you can be praying for him.
51. Spoil him.
52. Ask him to share his day first.
53. Make sure he knows he comes before the children.
54. Anticipate his needs.
55. Give him a huge hug and kiss every time you leave each other.
56. Believe in him.
57. Flirt with him.
58. Look into his eyes with an adoring smile.
59. Let 99 things go before you address one.
60. Approach problems with great gentleness and humility.

Project Self Denial

Self denial. These are two words we don't hear in every day conversation, do we? May I propose that's precisely the problem? We don't live these words because we don't like these words.

Every few months or so it seems the Lord impresses on me a new principle from God's Word that I am supposed to be living. So, I put the principle into a phrase that is easy for my little brain to remember. To remind me that God wants me to be content, that He's in charge, and to keep me from manipulating, I tell myself, "It is what it is." Then it's easier for me to let go and trust what God is doing.

To remind myself not to think more highly of myself than I ought or demand my way, I repeat the words, "Deny self, deny self." I encourage you to talk to yourself like I do! It might feel silly at first but it'll help you SO much as you remind yourself to live God's Word!

Denying self is contrary to everything in us, but it's certainly God's clear calling.

> *"And He was saying to them all, "If anyone wishes to come after Me, he must deny himself, and take up his cross daily and follow Me." Luke 9:23*

May God burn these truths into our hearts and make us vessels to be used mightily in the Master's hands.

Dear God, work a miracle of self denial in us!

The following is borrowed from the writings of my second favorite pastor, Dr. John MacArthur. (Of course, Rick's my favorite!)

Self Denial

When you are not forgiven or neglected, purposefully set at naught and you sting and hurt with the insult and oversight but your heart is happy because you have counted yourself to be worthy to suffer for Christ---
That is self denial.

When your good is evil spoken of, when your wishes are crossed, your advise disregarded, your opinions are ridiculed and you refuse to let anger rise up in your heart, when you take it all in patient loving silence---
That is self denial.

When you lovingly bear any disorder and irregularity or annoyance, when you can stand face to face with waste and folly and extravagance and spiritual insensitivity and endure it as Jesus endured it---
That is dying to self.

When you are content with any food, any offering, any clothes, any climate, any solitude, any society, any interruption by the will of God---
That is dying to self.

When you can never care to refer to yourself in conversation or to record your own good works or itch after commendation. When you can love being unknown---
That is dying to self.

When you see your (sister) prosper and honestly have her needs met and can rejoice with her in spirit and have no envy nor question God why your own needs are far greater and unmet---
That is dying to self.

When you can receive reproof and correction from one of lesser stature than yourself and humbly submit inwardly as well as outwardly, feeling no rebellion or resentment rising in your heart---
That is dying to self.

By John MacArthur

Heart-Work

Day Six
A Heart Devoted to My Husband

Please describe who God says you are by finishing the following sentence.
Then describe what that means.
I...

- Matthew 5:13

_____

_____

_____

- Matthew 5:14

_____

_____

_____

- John 1:12

_____

_____

_____

- John 10:27

_____

_____

_____

- John 10:28,29

_____

_____

_____

- John 15:5

_____ _____

_____ _____

- John 15:15

_____ _____

_____ _____

- John 15:16

_____ _____

_____ _____

- John 17:15

_____ _____

_____ _____

- John 17:21

_____ _____

_____ _____

- John 17:23

_____ _____

_____ _____

- John 17:24

_____ _____

_____ _____

Wow! Spend some time thanking God for His gigantic love for you!

Heart-Work

Day Seven
A Heart Devoted to My Husband

Please continue thinking about who God says you are. Please finish the same sentence as yesterday and describe what that means.
I ...

- Romans 6:7

_____
_____
_____

- Romans 6:11

_____
_____
_____

- Romans 6:18

_____
_____
_____

- Romans 8:11

_____
_____
_____

- Romans 8:37

_____
_____
_____

- Romans 8:38-39

_____

_____

_____

- 1 Corinthians 6:20

_____

_____

_____

- 2 Corinthians 3:5

_____

_____

_____

- 2 Corinthians 4:16

_____

_____

_____

- 2 Corinthians 5:17

_____

_____

_____

- 2 Corinthians 12:10

_____

_____

_____

**Work to replace wrong thoughts of yourself by
reviewing this lesson often!**

Heart-Work

Day Eight
A Heart Devoted to My Husband

Please continue thinking about who God says you are. Please finish the same sentence as yesterday and describe what that means.
I…

- Galatians 2:20

_____

_____

_____

- Ephesians 1:3

_____

_____

_____

- Ephesians 1:4

_____

_____

_____

- Ephesians 1:5

_____

_____

_____

- Ephesians 1:7

_____

_____

_____

- Ephesians 1:13

_____

_____

_____

- Ephesians 2:6

_____

_____

_____

- Ephesians 2:10

_____

_____

_____

- Ephesians 2:13

_____

_____

_____

Spend some time double checking with God that your "self esteem" is caught up in how great He is instead of how great you are or aren't.

Heart-Work

Day Nine
A Heart Devoted to My Husband

Please continue thinking about who God says you are. Please finish the same sentence as yesterday and describe what that means.
I…

- Philippians 1:6

_____

_____

_____

- Philippians 3:20

_____

_____

_____

- Philippians 4:13

_____

_____

_____

- Colossians 1:13

_____

_____

_____

- Colossians 2:10

_____

_____

_____

- Colossians 3:3

_____

_____

_____

- 1 Thessalonians 1:4

_____

_____

_____

- 2 Thessalonians 2:16

_____

_____

_____

- 2 Thessalonians 3:3

_____

_____

_____

**Pick one favorite truth from today's lesson
and carry it around with you all day.**

Heart-Work

Day Ten
A Heart Devoted to My Husband

Please continue thinking about who God says you are. Please finish the same sentence as yesterday and describe what that means.
I...

- 1 Timothy 6:17

_____

_____

_____

- 2 Timothy 1:7

_____

_____

_____

- Titus 3:5

_____

_____

_____

- Hebrews 3:1

_____

_____

_____

- Hebrews 7:25

_____

_____

_____

- 1 Peter 1:23

_____

_____

_____

- 1 Peter 2:9

_____

_____

_____

- 1 Peter 2:11

_____

_____

_____

- 2 Peter 1:3

_____

_____

_____

- 2 Peter 1:4

_____

_____

_____

- 1 John 1:7

_____

_____

_____

Sum up who you are in Christ. Please notice that Christ intends to complete you, not your husband.

Chapter Seven

Priority Number Three
A Heart Devoted to My Husband

Heart-Verse

*"Thy Word have I treasured in my heart,
That I might not sin against Thee."*

Psalm 119:11

Priority Number Three
A Heart Devoted to My Husband

I'm absolutely convinced that each of us has 100% control over our thoughts. Thankfully, God's Word overflows with clear commands for our thought life. I can choose to think negative, fearful, anxious thoughts or I can choose to think God's thoughts from His Word that are saturated with truth and will be encouraging, motivating and positive. It's a mental and emotional burden to think the worst of my husband or to accuse him of not loving or appreciating me enough. I don't want to go through the rest of my life with those crushing thoughts, do you?

Thankfully, our good, good Father will use His Word to help us get control of our minds again if they've fallen into an ugly pattern. If we're honest...we all need help gaining control of our thoughts. Our marriages depend on it and our mental health depends on it! If we can just get victory over the thoughts that feed us lies about our husbands, the rest will begin to fall into place.

I met with a woman recently who told me she had zero love for her husband. Even the sound of his voice irritated her. Instead of urging her to go find a good divorce attorney, I urged her to pray.

The simple act of telling God how you feel and that you've run out of love for your husband is the first step to radical change! Asking God to fill you with *His* love for your husband is a beautiful thing! He promises that He won't withhold any good thing from you, and loving your husband is a very good thing! It may take a little time and effort, but I'm certain that's a prayer God will answer.

Of course we run out of love sometimes! It shouldn't shock us that we're human and need God's constant love to fill our colanders. Thankfully all we have to do is go to God and ask Him to fill us with more. It's become a regular request in my prayer life.

So I reminded my friend that she's a colander in need of a fresh filling from her Heavenly Father. I promised her that He'd draw near to her as she drew near to Him and fill her to overflowing with His goodness and a new love for her husband. I also gently reminded her that love is based on fact, not feeling. Feelings can't be trusted, but that's another lesson for another book.

This week's homework has some of the verses God has used to control my thoughts and keep them holy and honoring to Him. May I suggest you copy these down on individual pieces of paper and tape them around your house where you will see them often? Ask the Holy Spirit to illumine these verses to your mind when ugly thoughts begin. Toss out the ugly ones and replace them with God's thoughts! And here's an added blessing... start hanging out with women who also think God's thoughts. I promise it will make your spiritual journey easier and lots more fun! Everything's better with godly girlfriends, right!?

Controlling our thoughts begins with *praying properly*. Pray the verses in your homework often, even daily, or hourly if necessary! Pray for victory over yucky thought patterns that have robbed your joy for too long.

Next, controlling our thoughts includes *thinking properly*. Think God's thoughts not Satan's thoughts! Replace old thought habits with new biblical habits. The easiest way to correct your old thoughts is to apply this week's verse and literally hide His Word in your heart! It'll be miraculous how meditating and memorizing His Word will change your thoughts, words and actions and give you joyful new habits between your earrings!

Finally, if you're praying properly and thinking properly, guess what!? You'll *live properly*...and that means you'll be pleasing to the Lord and a blessing to everyone who gets to bump into you today, especially your hubby!

Lord Jesus, here's a woman who longs to be released from the ugly, destructive thoughts that have kept her from enjoying the life You've given her. Please forgive her and help her to fill her mind with so much of You that she reflects Your sweetness, Your joy and Your tranquility to her husband first and to all those near her.
Do it Father, so that your dear Son would get all the glory,
For it's in His name I pray,
Amen

Day Eleven
A Heart Devoted to My Husband

Become a woman who is **focused on today!**

- Please write out Matthew 6:34.

_____

_____

_____

- Specifically, what is God asking you to think about/not think about?

_____

_____

_____

- Make a list of things that cause you to be anxious, worried, or fearful of the future.

_____

_____

_____

- Now write out your confession to God and ask Him to help you trust Him and focus on enjoying Him *this* day!

_____

_____

_____

How can I use this verse to bless my marriage?

Heart-Work

Day Twelve
A Heart Devoted to My Husband

Become a woman who **thinks happiness**!

- Please write out Philippians 4:8

_____

_____

_____

- Specifically, what is God asking you to think about/not think about?

_____

_____

_____

- Please summarize this verse in your own words.

_____

_____

_____

- List each of the opposite thoughts to this verse.

_____

_____

_____

Write a prayer asking the Holy Spirit to quickly convict you with this verse
whenever these opposite thoughts come into your mind.

_____

_____

_____

How can applying this verse bless my marriage?

Heart-Work

Day Thirteen
A Heart Devoted to My Husband

Become a woman who **anticipates the future**!

- Please write out Jeremiah 29:11

_____

_____

_____

Please explain this verse in your own words.

_____

_____

_____

- Please list as many observations as you can from this verse.

_____

_____

_____

- How can this verse bring me confidence and comfort?

_____

_____

_____

- Please take some time to ask God to help you think and rest in these words.

_____

_____

_____

How can using this verse bless my marriage?

Heart-Work

Day Fourteen
A Heart Devoted to My Husband

Become a **confident woman**!

- Please write out Romans 8:28

_____

_____

_____

- Please explain this verse in your own words.

_____

_____

_____

- How can you use this verse to control your mind?

_____

_____

_____

- Write a prayer to God using this verse. Pray this often.

_____

_____

_____

How can believing this verse bless my marriage?

Heart-Work

Day Fifteen
A Heart Devoted to My Husband

Become a woman who is **in awe of God**!

- Please write out Romans 11:33

_____

_____

_____

- What does this verse tell you about the ways of God?

_____

_____

_____

- How can thoughts of God help you control your mind.

_____

_____

_____

- Write a prayer telling God that you would rather have your thoughts elevated to thinking about Him than anything else.

_____

_____

_____

How can living this verse bless my marriage?

Chapter Eight

Priority Number Four
A Heart to Nurture My Children

Heart-Verse

*"I have no greater joy than this,
to hear of my children walking in the truth."*

3 John 1:4

Priority Number Four
A Heart to Nurture My Children

After all these years of studying Biblical parenting from the perfect Parent Himself, taking parenting courses, reading parenting books, watching other parents, and continual prayer, I'm still trying to fully grasp the principles I'll be sharing with you in this chapter. If there's any area of my life that I feel weight, responsibility and failure, it's in my parenting. God is faithful to use my children to show me my ugly and selfish heart. But it's also here, in my children's lives, that He shows me His great faithfulness to His Word and that's where I discover my most treasured blessings! To watch God illumine their hearts is utterly breathtaking!

The Preacher in Ecclesiastes gave specific direction for moms like us who can easily fear the uncharted waters of motherhood, he tells us to, "Fear God and keep His commandments." I'll try to give you a myriad of tips, principles, ideas and guidelines until your head swims with possibilities, all under the banner of "Fear God and keep His commandments." That's God's simple path to our highest goal of raising children who'll one day stand beside us in His presence.

Did you know the average mom spends less than 11 minutes a day meaningfully interacting with her children? And even worse, fathers spend less than 7 minutes a day with their children. Studies show that by age 10 or 12 most children have completely checked out from their parents. They don't need, care or desire their parents to have any part of their lives. How many people do you know that have children but have no desire to *be parents*? Sadly, many parents are completely absorbed in their own lives or they've withdraw out of fear and just let their children raise themselves. Parents often feel inadequate or just don't have the energy, so they make the grave mistake of parenting just for the moment. They yell, scream, belittle, hit, shame, or just give up.

God intends that we appropriate *His* grace as we parent *His* children. Since we can't lead our children where we haven't gone, we must live Deuteronomy 6. We must measure our parenting by His Word and not by the number of their involvements, brand name clothes, or straight A's. It's a lot easier to drop them off at practice (even though we complain about it) than to do the intentional and time consuming work it takes to know and train their hearts. What are we willing to invest to prepare the soil of their hearts in hopes that they'll come to love Jesus at the earliest possible age and walk with Him all their days?

Notes

_____
_____
_____
_____
_____
_____
_____
_____
_____
_____
_____
_____
_____
_____
_____
_____
_____
_____
_____
_____
_____
_____
_____

Project Aim

"She who aims at nothing hits it every time." Please! Let's not let that be true of our parenting! I know you have goals for your children, but maybe you haven't yet focused in and gotten intentional about them. Our project this week is to pray about what you want to aim for in your children's lives. List 5 Biblical character qualities you're aiming to produce in each of your children's lives, then write purposeful active steps you're going to take to make these aims realities. Include prayer in each goal; because we know without the Holy Spirit working in their hearts, no real change can occur. Use one sheet per child.

Goal #1 _____

* _____

* _____

* _____

Goal #2 _____

* _____

* _____

* _____

Goal #3 _____

* _____

* _____

* _____

Goal #4 _____

* _____

* _____

* _____

Goal #5 _____

* _____

* _____

* _____

Heart-Work

Day One
A Heart to Nurture My Children

Please read and ponder Psalm 27:4 for 10 or 15 minutes.

- What is the one thing David longs for?

_____

_____

_____

- Why?

_____

_____

_____

- Write a similar prayer for yourself.

_____

_____

_____

- Write a similar prayer for your child(ren).

_____

_____

_____

What is the "one thing" you're asking God to give you?

Heart-Work

Day Two
A Heart to Nurture My Children

Please record what God says about our children's hearts... (and ours!)

- Genesis 8:21

_____

_____

_____

- 1 Samuel 16:7

_____

_____

_____

- Hebrews 4:12

_____

_____

_____

- James 1:26

_____

_____

_____

- Psalm 51:10

_____

_____

_____

- Psalm 51:17

_____

_____

_____

- Psalm 119:11

_____

_____

_____

- Proverbs 4:23

_____

_____

_____

- Proverbs 20:5

_____

_____

_____

- Matthew 6:21

_____

_____

_____

What heart attitudes is God showing me in my children's lives?

What is my plan to guide their heart?

Heart-Work

Day Three
A Heart to Nurture My Children

Thoughtfully read Isaiah 29:13. Spend a few minutes getting a visual of it.

- What does God say He *does not* want from you or your children?

  _____

  _____

  _____

- What does this verse imply that God *does* want from you and your children.

  _____

  _____

  _____

- Do a heart check for yourself first, then your children…what do you see?

  _____

  _____

  _____

- Use this verse and write a prayer for yourself.

  _____

  _____

  _____

- Use this verse and write a prayer for your children.

  _____

  _____

  _____

Commit this issue to daily prayer with your children.

Heart-Work

Day Four
A Heart to Nurture My Children
What outward behaviors do we easily confuse with genuine saving faith?

- Matthew 19:16-21

_____
_____
_____

- Romans 1:21

_____
_____
_____

- Matthew 7:21-24

_____
_____
_____

- Luke 8:11-15, especially 13 and 14

_____
_____
_____

In this chapter, describe how Jesus feels about outward, hypocritical behavior.

- Matthew 23

_____
_____
_____

Plead with God, asking Him to root out any hypocrisy in your family.

Heart-Work

Day Five
A Heart to Nurture My Children

What outward behaviors confirm genuine saving faith?

- Psalm 32:5

_____

_____

- Psalm 42:1

_____

_____

_____

- Psalm 51:17

_____

_____

_____

- Psalm 115:1

_____

_____

_____

- James 5:16a

_____

_____

_____

- I John 3:14

_____

_____

_____

- James 4:4

_____

_____

_____

**Write a prayer that your children will walk with God
all the days of their lives and be a powerful tool in His hands to turn their
generation back to Him!**

Chapter Nine

Priority Number Four
A Heart to Nurture My Children

Heart-Verse

*"Children, be obedient to your parents in all things,
For this is well-pleasing to the Lord."*

Colossians 1:20

Priority Number Four
A Heart to Nurture My Children

What life stage are you in right now? Are you in the grandmother stage, encouraging your children and grandchildren? Or are you waiting patiently like Hannah for the motherhood stage? Are you secretly looking forward to the empty nest stage? Or maybe you're aching from a child who's just moved away and you're trying to wisely choose how to fill that void in your life? Life certainly has many stages doesn't it? As quoted in earlier pages, these words, scribbled in the back of my dear worn Bible has encouraged me *countless* times to not only focus on my present stage of life, but to relax and enjoy it!

C.A. Stoddards tells us, "We must say 'no' not only to things which are wrong and sinful, but to things that are pleasant and good which would hinder and clog our grand duties and our chief work."

I hope you're asking, "What *is* my grand duty and chief work?" If you'e in mommy stage your grand duty and chief work is to be the best, most fun, strict, silly, thoughtful, doting, biblical mom that ever walked the face of the earth! At least that's how I see it.

Take a moment and consider this, Satan wants you to fail as a mother. He wants you to get caught up in social media, soccer, piano lessons, exercising, your job, your friends, and any other justifiable "good thing" that'll keep you from precious time with your children. Doesn't mommy-ing take much more time and energy than you ever imagined? It requires immeasurable time for training, planning, consistent follow-through and unceasing prayer. The great J.C. Ryle warns our children of the enemy's desires for them,

"You are the prize for which he is especially contending. He foresees that you must either be a blessing or a curse in your day, and he is trying hard to gain entrance into your hearts, in order that you may help furthering his kingdom in the end."

Above all, we fight for our children's souls. We must not allow a day to pass without making spiritual deposits into their hearts. It may be opening the Word with them, it may be a sweet correction, or it may be a tearful reproof, but we must be diligent to invest Truth into their spiritual lives for we know it will never return void! The Holy Spirit will use it for the rest of their lives!

God speaks directly to our little ones in our key verse this week. "Children, be obedient to your parents in all things, For this is well-pleasing to the Lord."

It's a refreshingly clear, loving directive from the Lord to be obedient to the parents He sovereignly chose for them. The sooner they're able to grasp it, the sooner it'll save them untold heartache, and only that, but God says it pleases Him! How wonderful that our children can know that they're able to put a smile on their Heavenly Father's face!

It's binary. Either we're training these little souls for a life of submission or autonomy. Either were training them to please God or self.

I remember constantly reminding myself of the great spiritual rewards my children would one day reap if I both modeled a lifestyle of submission to God and required it of them. I feared the heartache that would lie ahead for them if they demanded to wear the red socks instead of the white ones I laid out for them at age 3. I tried to imagine what that behavior would turn into at age 10, 20 or 50. (Of course it's not about the socks! But it's the perfect window into their heart to see how willing they are to submit to me and ultimately the Lord!)

Autonomy leads to a lifestyle of rebellion. The Proverbs give serious warnings, "Do not be wise in your own eyes, fear God and turn away from evil," and "Do you see a man wise in his own eyes? There is more hope for a fool than for him."

Autonomy is the foolishness that's bound up in the heart of our children. It's part of mankind's fall into sin in Genesis 3. Remember how Eve decided to eat *on her own?* So it's our assignment by God, to drive it out of their hearts and nurture them to see that the only real joy in life will come from submitting everything to the One who'll lovingly care for their every need and bless them without measure!

Heavenly Father, give our children tender and obedient hearts. Gather them up in Your arms and love them as only You can so they will never be tempted to stray from You.
May Your nearness be their one desire.
Sanctify, enlighten, cheer and guide.
May they find all their delight in You.
Amen

How to Push Your Child Away

1. Have an unhappy marriage.
2. Discipline out of anger.
3. Constantly find fault.
4. Practice favoritism.
5. Give too much freedom.
6. Raise your voice.
7. Compare them to other children.
8. Withhold praise.
9. Break promises.
10. Be inconsistent.
11. Allow too many choices when they're young.
12. Allow not enough choices when they're older.
13. Maintain a child-centered home.
14. Speak harshly.
15. Never admit you are wrong.
16. Fail to listen carefully to them.
17. Make fun of them.
18. Expect too much.
19. Expect too little.
20. Rebuke them in front of others.
21. Reverse roles with your husband.
22. Intimidate.
23. Withhold physical affection.
24. Focus on outward behavior instead of their heart.
25. Be too busy to play or hang out with them.
26. Ignore them.
27. Call them to a higher standard than you are willing to meet.
28. Bring up past failures.
29. Manipulate.
30. Doubt them.
31. Fail to pray with them.
32. Don't cook for them.
33. Over-react.
34. Interrupt.
35. Know it all.
36. Be hard to please.
37. Abuse them physically.
38. Call them names.
39. Blame them.
40. Be legalistic.
41. Don't explain why.
42. Don't discipline Biblically.
43. Worry about what others think.

Project Evaluate

Please prayerfully evaluate how each of your children is demonstrating the following and list your plan to help them in each area.

1. Does my child truly understand the gospel message? (not, are they saved)

    How can I help my child understand the Gospel better?

2. Do I see the fruit of the Spirit displayed in my child? Galatians 5:22-23

    What can I do to encourage my child to live the fruit of the spirit?

3. Do I see a godly sorrow over sin?

    How can I explain the hatred God has for sin to my child?

4. Do I see a love for God and a hunger for His Word?

    What can I do to help my child fall in love with God's Word?

Heart-Work

Day Six
A Heart to Nurture My Children

• In Proverbs 8:11, what does God say is more important for your child than all else? _____
  Why?

  _____

  _____

• What does 13:18 say will happen if you neglect discipline?

  _____

  _____

• What does 13:24 say you will do if you hate your child?

  _____

  _____

• What does 13:24 say you will do if you love your child?

  _____

  _____

• What does 15:5 say a fool will do?

  _____

  _____

• When my child is young, what am I to do in 19:18?

  _____

  _____

Write a prayer for your child using today's lesson.

Heart-Work

Day Seven
A Heart to Nurture My Children

- In Proverbs 22:3, what do I want my child to do when he sees evil?

  _____

  _____

- What will happen to my child if I am faithful to train my child in 22:6?

  _____

  _____

- What is in my child's heart, 22:15?

  _____

  _____

- How does God say I can remove the above, 22:15?

  _____

  _____

- What does God warn me not to hold back from my child, 23:13

  _____

  _____

- What does God promise in 23:13?

  _____

  _____

**Ask God for courage to be annoyingly consistent
as you carry out today's lesson!**

Heart-Work

Day Eight
A Heart to Nurture My Children

- What happens if we don't deal with our child's transgressions?
  Proverbs 28:13

  _____

  _____

- What will the opposite bring in the same verse?

  _____

  _____

- What are the benefits of correcting your child? 29:17

  _____

  _____

- What does God say your child will do if you have been a diligent
  mother? 31:28

  _____

  _____

Ask God to burn His truths into your child's heart.

Heart-Work

Day Nine
A Heart to Nurture My Children

- In Ephesians 6:1, what does God say His will is for your children?

  _____

  _____

- How can your child show evidence of the above in the next verse?

  _____

  _____

- What does God say He will do in the next verse, if your child obeys you?

  _____

  _____

- In what things is your child to obey you? Colossians 3:20

  _____

  _____

- What does the next verse mean, Colossians 3:21?

  _____

  _____

- Do you ever do that? If so, please confess it now.

  _____

  _____

Ask God to help your child love obedience.

Heart-Work

Day Ten
A Heart to Nurture My Children

- List all the directives found in Hebrews 12:5-10?

  _____

  _____

  _____

  _____

- In verse 11, God knows discipline seems...

  _____

  _____

- Later in that verse, God says after we have been trained in discipline, we will be...

  _____

  _____

- What does discipline yield?

  _____

  _____

Thank God for being your perfect Parent and for His perfect example to us. Ask for His strength to love your child enough to discipline as He asks.

Chapter Ten

Priority Number Four
A Heart to Nurture My Children

Heart-Verse

"For I will give you abundant water for your thirst
And for your parched fields.
And I will pour out my Spirit
And my blessings on your children.

Isaiah 44:3

Priority Number Four
A Heart to Nurture My Children

It's so fitting that we close our lessons on children by focusing on prayer! All else matters little if we aren't mothers who "pray without ceasing," lifting our children to the throne of grace. We pray not because we want to, but because we must. We know that our countless acts of mothering love won't measure up to the love we display for them on our knees. We can wipe noses and bandage knees, but we can't make them love their Heavenly Father. Only God can light the fire of love for Him in their hearts. And only then, when our children's faith has laid hold of Christ, will our hearts know a measure of rest.

So many nights, I pleaded with God to let me just relax instead of put my little ones to bed. But He'd never let me off the hook. I had to get up and have some sweet conversation with them, then kneeling by their bed, I'd press my hands on their little bodies and let them listen while I prayed great big, gigantic prayers over them. And decades later, I'm still praying those prayers for them.

"When a mother prays for her wayward son,
No words can make clear the vivid reality of her supplications
She does not really think she is persuading God to be good to her son,
For the courage of her prayer is due to her certain faith that God also must wish that boy to be recovered from his sin.
She is rather taking on her heart the same burden that God has on His and is joining her demand with the divine desire.
In this system of personal life which makes up the moral universe,
she is taking her place alongside God in an urgent, creative outpouring of sacrificial love.
Her intercession is the utterance of her life; it is love on its knees."
Harry Emerson Fosdick

"I know not by what methods rare,
But this I know: God answers prayer.
I know not if the blessing sought
Will come in just the guise I thought,
I leave my prayer to Him alone
Whose will is wiser than my own."
Eliza M. Hickok

How to Keep Your Child Close

1. Laugh with them a lot.
2. Willingly say "I was wrong…will you forgive me?"
3. Celebrate everything.
4. Surprise them often.
5. Hold them close.
6. Kiss their whole face.
7. Listen actively.
8. Study God's Word together.
9. Affirm the little things.
10. Speak sweetly.
11. Pray with them.
12. Send them mail.
13. Appreciate everything.
14. Tuck them in bed.
15. Go on dates together.
16. Praise them in front of everyone.
17. Show your confidence in them.
18. Applaud biblical character in them.
19. Always have a huge smile for them.
20. Ask their opinion.
21. Tell them funny stories of your childhood.
22. Be happy.
23. Live your love for God openly.
24. Love and respect their father.
25. Offer help.
26. Dream with them about what God has in their future.
27. Get involved in their activities.
28. Make their favorite dinner.
29. Remind them what a blessing they are.
30. Share your life with them.
31. Play games.
32. Teach them what you know.
33. Honor their commitments.
34. Invite their friends over.
35. Let them see Christ in you.

Project Journal

Let's begin to journal our prayers for our children and grandchildren! Writing out our prayers will cause us to be more thoughtful and deliberate as we pray. It'll also be a precious reminder to Whom our children belong and keep us accountable to Him in our parenting.

Your child's prayer journal needs to have lists of concerns, aspirations, and biblical virtues you're asking God for. You can use a pretty new journal or an old spiral notebook. Some days you may write a short paragraph or bullet points and some days you may write several pages. Often your prayers will come from your daily study as you pray God's Word for your child.

You may also choose to journal prayers in your child's scrapbook or even send a prayer to your child occasionally as encouragement. You could also begin a collection of prayers for them to give them at their next birthday as one of my friends has encouraged me to do.

The goal is to pray, pray, pray. May this journal project be a great source of victory in your child's life and a great accountability tool! Regardless of their age, your children and grandchildren will be forever marked because you prayed for them!

I've often asked God to give my children the character of my Biblical heroes. I've prayed that God would give them Jesus's eyes to not only see the needs around them but the desire to act on those needs, like when Jesus talked to the outcast at the well or protected the woman from being stoned to death. I've asked God to give them Mary's humble faith when she prayed, "Behold the handmaid of the Lord," and Joshua's courage to rally others to trust God after he spied out the land.

Also, as you're looking for verses to add to your prayer journal, I suggest you write your children's initials by the verses you're praying for them. It's exciting to stumble across those verses again and again so you can keep praying God's Word for them!

May God richly reward you, Momma, as you storm heaven not just for blessings upon your children but for their impact for the Kingdom of Heaven!

Project Pray

May these biblical virtues be helpful prayer starters! Use them in your journal, post in their room or text them as blessings for your children or grandchildren!

1. Salvation, Acts 6:31
2. Understand God's love, Ephesians 3:18,19
3. Hunger for God's Word, Psalm 19:10
4. Desire for holiness, Ephesians 1:4
5. A servant's heart, Ephesians 6:7, Psalm 100:2
6. Wisdom beyond their years, Proverbs 13:1, 18:15, James 1:5
7. Quick to forsake sin, Isaiah 57:15
8. Courage to be a light in a dark world, Matthew 5:16, Luke 1:74,75
9. To love discipline, Hebrews 12:1-11
10. Hatred for sin, Psalm 51:1-9
11. Humility, 1 Peter 5:6, Titus 3:2
12. Self Control, Galatians 5:23
13. Merciful toward others, Matthew 5:7
14. Faithful in little things, Matthew 25:23
15. Joy, 1 Thessalonians 1:6
16. Godly spouse, Galatians 5:22,23
17. Protection, Hosea 2:6,7, Psalm 121:8
18. Contentment, Philippians 4:12,13
19. Walk with the wise, Proverbs 13:20
20. Look for opportunities to be a blessing, Galatians 6:10, Ephesians 2:10
21. Call on God, 1 Peter 5:7, Matthew 11:28
22. Obedience, Colossians, 3:20
23. Prosperous, 3 John 2, Psalm 115:14
24. Generous, Proverbs 11:25
25. Quick to forgive, Ephesians 4:32
26. Thankful, Ephesians 5:20, Colossians 2:7
27. Self Disciplined 1 Corinthians 9:24-27
28. Long for the Lord's return, Revelation 22:20
29. Teach others, 1 Corinthians 1:17,18, Colossians 3:16
30. Value Christ, Philippians 3:8

Heart-Work

Day Eleven
A Heart to Nurture My Children

To practice praying God's Word for your child/grandchild, please write a prayer for your child from each of these verses.

- Proverbs 2:10

  _____
  _____
  _____

- Matthew 5:13,14

  _____
  _____
  _____

- Ephesians 6:10

  _____
  _____
  _____

- Philippians 4:19

  _____
  _____
  _____

- Proverbs 3:6

  _____
  _____
  _____

- 1 Corinthians 13:5

  _____
  _____

Oh God, please answer this precious mother's prayers.

Heart-Work

Day Twelve
A Heart to Nurture My Children

To practice praying God's Word for your child/grandchild, please write a prayer for your child from each of these verses.

- Deuteronomy 28:1

  _____
  _____
  _____

- Romans 8:38,39

  _____
  _____
  _____

- Proverbs 3:7

  _____
  _____
  _____

- Proverbs 19:26

  _____
  _____
  _____

- 1 Thessalonians 3:12

  _____
  _____
  _____

- Proverbs 3:27

  _____
  _____

Oh God, please answer this faithful mother's prayers.

Day Thirteen
A Heart to Nurture My Children

To practice praying God's Word for your child/grandchild, please write a prayer for your child from each of these verses.

- 1 Corinthians 13:4,5

  _____

  _____

  _____

- Proverbs 1:8,9

  _____

  _____

  _____

- Psalm 17:8

  _____

  _____

  _____

- Proverbs 4:12

  _____

  _____

  _____

- Psalm 37:26

  _____

  _____

  _____

Oh God, please honor these precious prayers.

Heart-Work

Day Fourteen
A Heart to Nurture My Children

To practice praying God's Word for your child/grandchild, please write a prayer for them from each of these verses.

- Ephesians 6:11

  _____
  _____
  _____

- Galatians 6:9

  _____
  _____
  _____

- Luke 6:38

  _____
  _____
  _____

- Proverbs 6:22

  _____
  _____
  _____

- Psalm 60:12

  _____
  _____
  _____

- Ephesians 1:18

  _____
  _____

Oh God, please answer these precious prayers.

Heart-Work

Day Fifteen
A Heart to Nurture My Children

To practice praying God's Word for your child/grandchild, please write a prayer for them from each of these verses.

- 2 Corinthians 9:8

_____

_____

_____

- Ephesians 6:4

_____

_____

_____

- Psalm 23:1

_____

_____

_____

- Romans 12:10

_____

_____

_____

- Romans 12:12

_____

_____

_____

- Psalm 86:12

_____

_____

Oh God, please answer this wonderful mom's prayers.

Chapter Eleven

Priority Number Five

A Heart Burning For Others

Heart-Verse

"…but whoever wishes to become great among you
Shall be your servant,
And whoever wishes to be first among you
Shall be your slave;
Just as the Son of Man did not come to be served,
but to serve,
And to give His life a ransom for many."

Matthew 20:26-28

Priority Number Five
A Heart Burning For Others

Whose life are you changing?
Whose life have you blessed today?
Who are you sharing the gospel with?
Who has God laid on your heart to pray for?
Who is hurting today that you can comfort?
Who are you pouring your life into?
Who are you getting to know?
Who have you encouraged?
Who have you loved?

These are questions I ask myself regularly. I know how self-absorbed I can be. I've learned the hard way how miserable and depressed I get when I don't have the joy of serving others.

The substance of our walk with God will be seen in our attitude toward serving others. The better question might be, "Do we even know there *are* others?"

Let's look at Jesus. His life was consumed by others. He continually fed, healed and taught multitudes. Mobs chased Him...not because they loved Him, but because He had something to offer. They wanted Him only to take from Him. (Ever feel like that!?)

Jesus hid to have private time in prayer only to be hunted down. He tried to get alone with His disciples on a boat and the crowds were waiting for Him when He docked the boat on the other side. Did it stop Him? Did He quit because He was used and unappreciated? No way. He continued to give and give and give until in the end He gave even His life.

Notice the kind of people Jesus loved. Many were stinking with rotting flesh, others were blind or crippled, prostitutes or beggars. He came for those who were homeless and hungry and hated. He came for those who needed Him most. He came for us.

Have you ever sat down by someone with a mental disability and loved them like Jesus would? Have you ever started a conversation with someone in a wheelchair, or fed a homeless stranger?

If we are "Christians" who are "like Christ" aren't we to be here for those who need us most? Shouldn't our lives be an offering to His example?

I'm convicted that Jesus never had to write, "Do an act of kindness" on His schedule so He wouldn't forget. He didn't need a reminder to think of others. Should I be any different?

Rick and I have been inspired by many great men who have given their lives so completely to God and to others, that they've actually died of exhaustion. They wore out their bodies and died early in life because they were compelled to love others as Jesus did. That's our goal. If we can't be martyred for Christ, we want to choose the honorable death of 'wearing out' for Christ.

Sadly, my sense of 'otherness' can too often be congratulated by sending a few dollars to orphans in a far away land where I won't have to be touched by their dirty hands, or wounded by their sad eyes. Sometimes, without realizing it, we demand distance if we are going to serve others. We'd never let a bloody woman touch our clothing or a prostitute wash our feet. How often would we sit back and be content with the 99, while He's going after the one who's lost their way? Do we go after the one? Or have we even noticed they're gone?

I wonder how my heart will stand the piercing one day, when I see disappointment in His eyes for the missed opportunities He gave me to love His unlovely ones. O, I need God to give me the eyes of Christ! I need eyes open wide to see the needs He has placed right in front of me. Do you? Let's move through the crowd, through the office, through the classroom touching, noticing, smiling, asking, just like Jesus did. Every single morning may our waking thoughts be asking God, "Use me!"

"Make us like Jesus with no thought of ourselves, no need for pillow or comfort, only the need to be spilled out as an offering to those who need You. May we be found pulling and dragging them to You to heal their broken hearts.
For Jesus sake,
Amen"

Notes

_____

_____

_____

_____

_____

_____

_____

_____

_____

_____

_____

_____

_____

_____

_____

_____

_____

_____

_____

_____

_____

Project Care

I wonder if you're like me and have all kinds of wonderful intentions to show love and concern for others, but get stuck in knowing how to add more to our already busy lives. I've compiled a few practical ways we can show everyday love and care. May these simple things be reminders to us to live like Jesus, with eyes to see that those around us need a loving touch. If these are difficult for you please go back and study Priority One and Two.

1. Look others in the eyes and smile, smile, smile.
2. Send 3 sentence appreciation notes.
3. Give compliments to everyone, including strangers.
4. Invite someone new to lunch.
5. Ask, "How can I pray for you?"
6. Find the new girl and ask her to sit by you.
7. Be a great listener.
8. Let down your walls.
9. Share the dumb thing you did yesterday.
10. Don't worry about what others think of you.
11. Ask God to make you a blessing.
12. Throw your opinions out the window.
13. Throw your expectations out the window.
14. Show your appreciation for the smallest things.
15. Assume others need you. Not the other way around.
16. Laugh at yourself.
17. Enjoy the differences in others, don't try to fix them.
18. Befriend someone needy and unlovely.
19. Have 1,000 best friends.
20. Send silly or thinking of you, emails and texts.
21. Bake cookies or freezer meals for a busy or sick acquaintance.
22. Introduce yourself first.
23. Ask, "So what's going on in *your* life?"
24. Be happy.
25. Use these words often, "I am so proud of you!"

Project Serve

Please take some time to prayerfully evaluate your heart for others, your acts of kindness, and the sweetness you show to others for Jesus sake.
How are you doing?

1. How can you be more like Christ in seeing and feeling compassion for those near you?

   What steps can you take to improve?

2. What is keeping you from serving and loving others more?

   What are you going to do about it?

3. How concerned are you about the needs of others compared to your own needs?

   Is there room for improvement?

4. If I concern myself with the needs of others, who'll take care of mine?

Heart-Work

Day One
A Heart Burning For Others

Please explain what is God asking of us in the following verses.

- Proverbs 11:25

  _____

  _____

- James 1:27

  _____

  _____

- Matthew 5:38-46

  _____

  _____

- Acts 20:35

  _____

  _____

- Isaiah 35:3

  _____

  _____

- 1 Thessalonians 5:14

  _____

  _____

- 2 Timothy 2:21

  _____

  _____

What one area can you specifically ask God for help?

Heart-Work

Day Two
A Heart Burning For Others

How can you live what God is asking of you in these verses?

- Leviticus 25:35

_____

_____

- Romans 15:2

_____

_____

- Colossians 3:16

_____

_____

- 1 Samuel 12:23

_____

_____

- Nehemiah 1:1-11

_____

_____

- Hebrews 6:10

_____

_____

- Titus 3:1

_____

_____

- 1 Timothy 6:18

_____

_____

Ask for His compassionate eyes to see the needs around you.

Heart-Work

Day Three
A Heart Burning For Others

What is God telling you?

- Ephesians 2:10

  _____

  _____

- 2 Timothy 3:17

  _____

  _____

- Titus 3:14

  _____

  _____

- Acts 9:36

  _____

  _____

- 2 Corinthians 9:8

  _____

  _____

- Hebrews 10:24

  _____

  _____

- Matthew 6:1

  _____

  _____

- Titus 2:14

  _____

  _____

Ask God to let you be His vessel to love others through.

Heart-Work

Day Four
A Heart Burning For Others

What can you apply from these verses?
- John 21:15-17

_____

_____

- John 13:34

_____

_____

- Romans 12:10

_____

_____

- 1 Corinthians 10:24

_____

_____

- 1 Peter 2:17

_____

_____

- 1 Thessalonians 5:12,13

_____

_____

- Leviticus 19:34

_____

_____

- John 13:35

_____

_____

**What attitude changes do you need to make so you can
love and serve others better?**

Heart-Work

Day Five
A Heart Burning For Others

Describe what Jesus does and the feelings He displays.

- Matthew 11:28-30

  _____

  _____

- Isaiah 40:11

  _____

  _____

- Hebrews 2:18

  _____

  _____

- Luke 7:11-15

  _____

  _____

- Matthew 14:14

  _____

  _____

- Matthew 9:36

  _____

  _____

- Luke 19:41

  _____

  _____

Ask God to give you a heart like His that burns for others.

Conclusion

Before I let you spin your chair around and look in the mirror at all God has transformed in your life, I have one last beauty tip to leave you. It's very important to me that you take this to heart.

I know you feel you're insignificant. I know you often wonder if you, or anything you do really matters. I know your best efforts often go unnoticed and you sometimes wonder why you even bother trying.

Dearest sister, I want you to take a moment and try to grasp your preciousness to God! I want you to be overwhelmed that the Great God of Heaven not only sees you and thinks of you but *has set His heart on you!* He thinks of you as more precious than all the earth's treasures. His thoughts of you are more numerous than the sands of the sea. His love grasps you securely, and will never end.

> *"How precious are Thy thoughts unto me, O God!*
> *How great is the sum of them. If I should number them,*
> *They would out number the sand.*
> *When I awake, I am still with Thee."*
> *Psalm 139:17, 18*

Before the foundations of the world He chose to love you and draw you close to Him. His Infinite Mind is drawn around you closer than a mother holds her newborn baby. There's not a moment He isn't thinking of you and graciously working His loving will for your good.

> *"I know the thoughts I think towards you, saith the LORD;*
> *Thoughts of peace and not evil, to give you an expected end."*
> *Jeremiah 29:11*

Your family may neglect you. Your friends may forget you. The crowds may pass you by and you may feel alone, but dear one, God cannot and will not. He tells you that even though a mother may forget her nursing child, He will not forget you. *You are engraved on the palms of His Hands. (Psalm 49:16)*

His love for you is so complete, and so costly He sacrificed His own precious Son to buy you, and adopt you as His very own. When you came to Him as a beggar, He swept your sins away and clothed you with Christ's own stunning righteousness. His Fatherly love even now is preparing a new and gorgeous home for you, because He longs for you to be near Him forever.

Puritan writer, Octavious Winslow, tells us...

"Have you relinquished some fond idol, or mortified some darling sin,
or resisted some potent temptation,
or discharged some act of self denial for the honour of His name?
God thinks of it.
Every habit you lay down, or cross you take up or burden you bear,
or yoke to which you bow for Jesus,
shall be treasured in the thoughts of thy God through eternity."

He sees what you have given up for Him! He treasures each choice you make that puts Him first in your heart. Each struggle you make to be like Christ is a sweet gift of love for Him.

Please, my friend, the next time you're swallowed up by your own sinfulness and unworthiness, remember, His "thoughts are not your thoughts". Trace back the streams of blessing in your life to the unspeakably loving heart of God and rest with Him there. "Cast your cares on Him, for He cares for you." Let Him give you comfort as you fix your mind on Him. Let Him soothe and refresh you with His overwhelming love. Know that He is using all these things to lead you closer still.

"He will call upon Me, and I will answer him;
I will be with him in trouble;
I will rescue him and honor him.
With long life I will satisfy him,
And let him behold my salvation."
Psalm 91:15,16

Now my work is done. I can't wait to meet with you again for another study on another topic. Keep living what we've learned together! Let everyone in your life see and enjoy your Extreme Spiritual Makeover, your beautiful reflection of Christ and His priorities for your life!

About the Author

Kris is committed to serving women's ministries in churches worldwide. Her passion for knitting women's hearts to the heart of God makes her an excellent choice as a women's conference and retreat speaker. Her energy is contagious, her Bible teaching, fresh and practical. Women are drawn to Kris's love for her Savior and her enthusiasm for life.

Kris has faithfully served alongside her husband in Birmingham, New Orleans, Los Angeles and Kansas. Along the way Kris has taken classes at Southeastern Bible College and completed the Seminary Wives course at The Master's Seminary. God granted her outstanding success in business, including dressing Hollywood's elite. She had the marvelous privilege to be personally discipled by her dear friend and lifelong mentor, Elizabeth George.

Together, Rick and Kris have had the joy of over 34 years in ministry to God's people all over the world. Their local ministry is based at Shades Mountain Community Church in Birmingham, AL where Rick is the Lead Pastor and Kris is the Women's Ministry Director. Most important to her are the three joys of her life, named Bethany, Sarah, and Joshua and their growing families.

Certainly you've felt Kris' love and commitment to you from spending these weeks studying with her. If this study has blessed your life, Kris would love to hear from you! Please reach out to her on Facebook, email, or visit her at her website so she can rejoice with your Extreme Spiritual Makeover!

Please continue reflecting Christ in all you do!

Kris Goertzen

website: www.krisgoertzen.com
email: info@krisgoertzen.com

Made in the USA
Coppell, TX
16 January 2022

71736021R00085